The Apostle Paul writes in 2 Corinthia~   ur
affliction and with that same comf~
you will find gospel-centred c
loss of his wife. The book i.   .ated
with Scriptures. It will both t.   .ow to walk
with those who are passing thr.   ueath. This book
is a gift to the church so pick up ぇ   .riend.

Andy Constable, pastor at Niddri   *..rch and the Principal of the*
Ragged School of 1.   , ぇ 20schemes ministry in Scotland.

Gripping, raw and real, written in the midst of intense suffering, this book is a
rare treasure. Brad is a gentle guide, sharing practical and yet profound ways that
we can turn to God in our grief.

**Linda Allcock is the author of Deeper Still: Finding Clear Minds and Full Hearts
through Biblical Meditation, and Head, Heart, Hands Bible notes, and works
alongside her husband Jonty, at The Globe Church, Central London.**

With honesty (sometimes searing) and transparency (often searching), Brad
Franklin opens his soul about the experience of suddenly losing his beloved wife,
and all that is involved in such a grief. The human side of the story is on careful,
painful display; the divine side—known and unknown—is consistently and sweetly
emphasised ... God's truth is on realistic display, whether objectively declared or
subjectively enjoyed, in the heights and depths of Christian experience. Anyone
who knows precisely the same grief will find much to comfort and instruct them
here. Those whose griefs are somewhat removed will still find a blessing as they
seek to navigate the shade and light of a life lived in the aftermath of death. My
heart often ached, my tears regularly fell, and my soul occasionally soared as I
read my friend's words. I trust they will do you the same kind of good.

Jeremy Walker, pastor of Maidenbower Baptist Church, Crawley.

On one level this is a book about an everyday, earthy, real family living in north London through a heartbreaking tragedy. On another level, it is this family's life from the vantage point of heaven, in the light of the eternal world and through the lens of the sovereignty and providence of God. The story itself is remarkable and moving, but the way Brad tells it, makes it a real page turner. By the end of the book I was compelled to say, 'How good is the God we adore'.

Alun Ebenezer, Founding Headmaster of The Fulham Boys School, where three (or is it four now) of Brad's sons are students.

Grief is raw: Job chapter 3 makes that plain. But it can also be godly, as we see in Job chapters 1 and 2. Brad's book is tough and tender – both in the story he tells and in his call for us to grieve well. So much of Brad's wisdom is applicable to all of life, not just grieving, and his description of God's support through the local church is so heart-warming. Honest, biblical, hopeful ... this may be exactly what you need to hear, from someone who has been through the storm.

Phil Heaps, co-pastor, Highbury Baptist Church.

Brad Franklin could scarcely have faced a greater storm. He writes these haunting words: 'On 31st December I received word that my wife, the mother of my seven children, would almost certainly die.' And he describes to us what it is to have the roof of God's sovereignty 'on'. He and his family have paid a huge price to write this book. Its hard-won theological, practical and emotional wisdom is incalculable.

Rico Tice, Senior Minister, Evangelism, All Souls.

A Guide for Glorifying God through the
Loss of a Loved One

when
sorrows
like sea
billows
roll

By
Brad Franklin

Grace
Publications

Grace Publications Trust
62 Bride Street
London N7 8AZ
www.gracepublications.co.uk

First Published in Great Britain by Grace Publications Trust in 2023

Cover design by Pete Barnsley (CreativeHoot.com), with thanks to James Garnham for the initial concept.

ISBN Paperback: 978-1-912154-81-4
       Ebook: 978-1-912154-82-1

Printed and bound in Great Britain by Ashford Colour Press.

Note from the author: After Horatio Spafford wrote the hymn 'It Is Well With My Soul', it appears he strayed from Christian orthodoxy. Notwithstanding, I decided that the hymn was written by a man – who at least at the time – was holding to more biblical convictions than he later espoused. The fact is, he produced a piece of poetry that is wonderful – practically and theologically. As such, I believe this hymn is worth knowing, singing and learning from today.

This book is lovingly dedicated to the elders and members of St Giles Christian Mission.

Contents

Foreword

There are books about grief that are written in a kind of abstract way, books that look to the Bible to examine what it says about the source of our pain and sorrows or to suggest how God may use them in the lives of his people. Such works have their place and can be good and helpful. I have often benefitted from them.

But in our hardest moments and darkest valleys, we often find ourselves looking for a different kind of book – one written by someone who has already endured a deep sorrow and who is now reflecting on it. This kind of book teaches truth and provides encouragement, but does so in the form of narrative.

When Sorrows Like Sea Billows Roll is very much that kind of a book. Brad Franklin tells of the sudden, unexpected, grievous loss of his wife, and, as he does so, tells how God was present, how God helped him, and what he learned about God as they walked together through the Valley of the Shadow of Death. He describes how he applied the truths of Scripture to his situation and how he endured his loss with many tears and much sorrow, but also with faith, hope, and even joy.

And as he does all of this, he serves as a kind of guide who can help others as they endure the sorrows they may face as they make the long and often sad journey through this life. That makes this an experienced, compassionate, realistic, and helpful work that can and, I trust, will serve many. It comes with my highest recommendation.

Tim Challies, February 2023

i

when sorrows like sea billows roll

Introduction

Tortilla chips

I wish I could go back to the 28th of December. It was my last proper night with Megan, and we spent the evening together on a hospital ward. She sat on the bed, and I sat on the chair beside her. We spoke about, of all things, tortilla chips.

Our conversation that night reflected our expectations. We *expected* Megan to be out of hospital soon. So we spent our evening discussing our grocery delivery. We set out the week's menu and spent a special amount of time planning the food for our annual New Year's Eve 'open house.'

You see, the year before, we'd forgotten the tortilla chips, which forced me into a frantic search across London. Who would have thought that every shop in our area would be sold out? But they were. And there we were, laughing about it all a year later.

It's both sad and ironic that our family ended up eating a lot of tortilla chips over the next few days. It's a gross understatement, but things didn't go quite as planned. Nothing those days really did.

Let me back up a bit. While we sat in hospital, Megan was seven months pregnant with our seventh child. We already had five boys and a girl, and we eagerly anticipated the arrival of another boy. We'd welcomed a child almost every two years. Our lives were happily full at home and with gospel ministry. I was then (and still am) serving as one of the pastors of a church in north London. The Christmas period is normally a busy and exciting time, full of carol singing, gingerbread houses, nativity plays, and turkey dinners.

That Christmas morning, the children and I drove Megan to hospital. For a few days, she'd had crippling headaches, and that morning it was more than she could handle. The headaches hurt, but the blurry vision was frightening. The doctors gave us an early diagnosis: pregnancy-induced migraines. That seemed reasonable. So I preached my Christmas morning sermon, and then the children and I had a subdued Christmas dinner. We sent Megan photos of the Christmas pudding she'd made, and we even saved a bit for her. Over the next few days, Megan was in and out of hospital. The headaches didn't really improve. On the 28th, the doctors decided she should stay under observation.

That night, Megan had a fitful night's sleep. Her headaches were too much for her, and the ward was anything but quiet. We spoke briefly on the phone the next morning, and she was desperate for sleep. Who could blame her? At home, our morning plans continued, as of yet, unabated. I took our 13-year-old to the GP's. He had tonsillitis, and needed antibiotics.

When I got back home, I got a phone call that nobody ever wants to receive: get to hospital as soon as possible. Megan

2

was in a bad way, and she wanted me there. I shudder anytime I remember that moment. Hastily organising childcare, I rushed down to the hospital. When I got there, mercifully, she was asleep. 'Yes,' I thought. 'Just what she needs.' I quietly sat at her bedside on the same uncomfortable chair I'd occupied the night before.

I couldn't have been there longer than five minutes before everything changed.

In an instant, Megan sat up and half-asked, half-mumbled for a pillow. Her neck hurt – or at least that's what I concluded from her pointing.

Have you ever had one of those moments where life just seems to be happening around you? You're there, but you seem to be looking in from the outside? It may sound cliched, but that's what happened to me. Within seconds, Megan's bed was surrounded – there must have been ten people there – nurses, doctors, strangers.

One of them pulled me aside: Megan wasn't breathing. They didn't know why. They rushed her to critical care so that they could stabilise her and begin running tests. I was urged to call our family and friends, and then meet Megan there in an hour. I phoned family in America and friends across the UK. I needed help. I needed prayer. I didn't really know what I needed.

All of this happened on the afternoon of December 29th. And so began a climactic week in hospital for us all. In the early hours of the 30th, our sixth son was safely delivered by Caesarean. Delivering him, the doctors believed was the best course of action as it allowed them to more actively care for

Megan. There I was: the proud father of seven. I went to see the wee one soon after. He was well, even though his mummy wasn't.

I was torn in two – overjoyed, but distraught. Full of joy at the birth of our son, yet full of fear at Megan's precarious state. Now, our attention turned to Megan.

She continued to be heavily sedated and on life support. Early scans showed severe swelling of the brain. That was a blow. Of course, this generated all sorts of questions: How bad was the damage? What had caused it? Would she recover? The first 36 hours in critical care answered the first question: the damage to Megan's brain was, in the words of the registrar: 'catastrophic.' The early signs for survival, let alone recovery, were grim. Another day of tests didn't lead to better news. On the 31st of December, we were told that, barring a miracle, Megan would die.

We still didn't know the cause of the swelling, but we nonetheless began to pray for a miracle. Our God created the world by His powerful word, calmed the storm with a word, healed the blind, and, himself a man, rose from the dead on the third day. Our God is more than capable of healing catastrophic bodily conditions. So we prayed, and we waited.

A few days later, we learned the cause of the swelling: Megan had a bacterial infection through, of all things, a scrape on her knee. It sounds ridiculous – unbelievable, really – but it's true. We knew when and where Megan had scraped her knee: a few weeks earlier, on the night of our church's carol and nativity service. She'd slipped on the stairs.

Over the days that followed, Megan had managed the minor wound. It had started to look a bit infected, but we'd thought nothing of it. Now we saw things in a different light. We were floored – so much damage done by such a small scrape. Still, we prayed, and we waited.

Those seven days Megan spent on the critical care ward were touch-and-go. I spent nearly all my waking hours at hospital. I didn't want to leave Megan's side, in case there might be some change or some news. Quite literally, I spent an entire week walking between Megan's bedside and the critical care 'relatives' room. I only left the ward for meals. Kind nurses from neonatal intensive care regularly brought the baby to see Megan and I on the ward. We cherished those times. Megan 'held' our little guy, and I talked to both of them.

Megan remained in a medically induced coma. Nonetheless, a number of brothers in Christ came by to spend time with us; their presence encouraged me. We spent the days together, and, other dear friends (usually couples) sat by Megan's bedside through the night, so that I could try to get some rest. It was a hard week.

The miracle we prayed for that week didn't happen. Megan wasn't recovering. And then things got worse. The neurologists conducted further assessments, and the results were conclusive: the swelling had so severely damaged Megan's brain stem that there was no basic brain function – no heartbeat, no breathing. She would never again regain consciousness. Megan only appeared to be breathing because the ventilator kept her lungs pumping and her heart beating.

Under the direction of the doctors and recognising God's sovereign will, we made the grave decision to turn off the life support. Before doing so, we gave friends and family a final opportunity to say 'goodbye.' We were overwhelmed by their love and support.

A day later, ten or so of us squeezed into the light blue curtained cubicle surrounding Megan's bed. Megan seemed to be merely sleeping, but the tubes connected to her body told another story. There were weak smiles and lots of hugs. The critical care ward seemed a sterile place for such a moment, but there we were. After singing a hymn and having a brief time of prayer, we turned off the machinery. The beeps and the hisses, ever-present over that last week, were strangely silent. In that little cubicle, we expressed our thanks to God for Megan's life even as we mourned her death.

She really was gone. Some remained for some time; others went back home.

A mere eight days after our tortilla chips chat, Megan was gone. Our beloved wife, amazing mum, devoted daughter, and faithful sister was no longer with us. At home, it was me and our now seven children.

*****

Inward desolation

What I've just done is give you our family's story and the background to all that follows. What I didn't do, really, is tell you how much it all *hurt* – both in that week and in all the days since. I may have hinted at it, and we certainly will get to it. Snapshots from that time come to mind, and I *feel* them still. I'm not sure I would have used the word at the time, but we were grieving.

What is grief? JI Packer's definition is helpful:

> It can be safely said that everyone who is more than a year old knows something of grief by firsthand experience, but a clinical description will help us to get it in focus. Grief, then, is the inward desolation that follows the losing of something or someone we loved – a child, a relative, an actual or anticipated life partner, a pet, a job, one's home, one's hopes, one's health or whatever.[1]

Inward desolation. That puts words to how I felt, how we felt. Our world had been rocked to the core. Everything looked and felt different. Over time, this inner feeling has been accompanied by all the usual realities: tears, shock, exhaustion, discouragement. We were grieving. We are grieving.

A grief observed, a help desired

Thank you, whoever you are. Somehow a copy of CS Lewis' A *Grief Observed* ended up in my hands shortly after Megan's death[2]. I got a lot of gifts like that around that time. Humorously,

---

1   J.I. Packer, A *Grief Sanctified: Love, Loss and Hope in the Life of Richard Baxter*, SPCK Publishing, 1998, pg 11. Packer's book on Richard Baxter's bereavement is well worth a read. Though focusing on Baxter, Packer compares CS Lewis' writings on grief with Baxter's writings on grief. The comparison is edifying, and it encouraged me in the writing of this book.

2 C.S. Lewis, A *Grief Observed*, Faber and Faber Limited, 1961

I already had a tatty, old copy on my shelf that, I admit, I hadn't read. So I welcomed a pristine, new copy. I managed to finish it within a few months or so after Megan's death.

The book offers an account of Lewis' experience following the death of his wife, Joy. They were only married for a brief period, but Lewis was profoundly affected by her death. It's a good book – useful in all the ways Lewis is always useful. He reflects so well on human experience, and then he manages to put things so well. Lewis felt Joy's death, and he describes it painfully and beautifully.

And yet, I was left wanting more. I didn't necessarily want more from Lewis. How dare I presume to say CS Lewis fell short? That thought might get me in trouble with some! His book accomplished what he set out to do.

What I wanted was *more* help in my grief. What do I mean? Let's liken grief following a bereavement to a storm at sea. In *A Grief Observed*, Lewis describes the storm. You can see and even feel the wind and the waves crashing against the boat. But I needed more help to find my way *through* the storm. I wanted someone to direct me towards land, someone to remind me how to steer the ship, and someone to give me hope even if I felt like I might never make it. Lewis wrote a travelogue through a storm with an eye to God. I wanted a God-centred travel guide through storms. I wanted comfort in light of the gospel of Jesus Christ. I wanted (and needed!) truths to direct my thinking according to Scripture. I wanted Biblical direction on how to live with and through grief in a way that honours God.

I needed help to grieve *better*, in a 'manner worthy of the gospel' (Phil. 1:27). Even in our sorrows – perhaps especially in our sorrows – we can grieve *better*.

To some, this idea will be offensive. 'How dare I dictate how anybody *should* grieve?! Grieving is very personal.' To pick up our storm at sea image again, many feel that in our journey through grief we are at the whim of the wind and the waves. You must simply go where the storm takes you. Grief may be a process, but it can't necessarily be directed. There's some truth to this, but don't sailors want to sail *well* through a storm? A sailor wants to actively steer the boat as best he can, setting up the boat (and any passengers) to survive (and maybe even thrive) in the storm.

The idea of comparing grief to a storm at sea isn't original to me. It's God's idea – more on that later on. Between the Bible and today though, many have used this image. Perhaps none more memorably than Horatio Spafford. His story is well known to many: shortly after losing his fortune in a fire and his son to scarlet fever, Spafford lost his remaining four children in a shipwreck. In his grief, he powerfully wrote a hymn with the counter-intuitive title: 'It Is Well With My Soul.' Somehow, he penned these words:

> When peace like a river attendeth my way
> When sorrows like sea billows roll
> Whatever my lot, thou hast taught me to say
> It is well, it is well with my soul

Spafford had been *taught* to grieve well. That's what I want this book to do for you.

Obviously, then, the idea of grieving well isn't original to me. It's God's idea. To quote a famous passage: 'Brothers and sisters, we do not want you to be uninformed about those who sleep in death, so that you do not grieve like the rest of mankind, who have no hope' (1 Thes. 4:13). Quite simply, God wants his people to grieve a particular way. A different way than the world grieves. A way that's founded on, or a response to, our hope in Christ.

It's this distinctly Christian grieving that this book aims at. I want to help you sanctify your grieving. I want to offer you the help I myself wanted and needed. I want to grieve better. I want to help you grieve better. I want us to look more and more like Jesus through our grief, and perhaps even because of our grief. I want to teach you to say: 'It is well with *my* soul.' Every writer says this, I know, but I don't know of another book quite like the one you're holding.

What you have in your hands is a reflection upon the death of my wife and our family's experiences around and since that time. But this is not purely a memoir. This book is a God-centred travel guide through grief. Its thesis: we can not only survive but thrive through the loss of our loved ones. We can and should become more like Christ in our sorrows. We can learn how to say 'It is well with my soul.'

Mourning with those who mourn

This book is written for our seven children. Of course, I don't expect them *all* to read it, at least not yet. But I hope they will one day. I want to explain to our children how I thought about and how I grieved over their mum's death. I want to convey to them my deep love for Megan, and my enduring hope beyond her grave. I want to help them miss their mummy and yet respond well to her death. I want to instil in them a love for and faith in Jesus Christ. I want them to grieve *well*. I want them to say: 'It is well with my soul.'

Of course, this book is not merely for my children, this book is also for me. That's right. I began writing in the days around and after Megan's death purely for the benefit of my own soul. Some of these reflections have their beginning in a series of messages I wrote during the time. I've continued to write up till the present.

Though it's been more than four years, I'm still grieving Megan's death. I still miss her. I ache for her almost every day. I wanted to capture how I felt, and then I wanted to direct myself back to the Bible. I told friends at the time I wasn't sure if my writings would ever see the light of day. I was 'ok' with that. I wrote what I wrote because I want to be more like Jesus. I want to grieve *well*. I am saying and want to keep saying: 'It is well with my soul.'

Lastly, of course, I also wrote this for you, whoever you are. This book is for anyone who mourns. Anyone who is grieving the death of a loved one. Anyone who is sad because of all the varied sufferings of life 'under the sun' (Ecc. 1:3). If this is you, right now, please see in this book my desire to help you. I'm not trying to tell you how to grieve 'properly' or beat you over the head with biblical principles. Through this travel guide, even through my missteps, I want you to see Jesus. It's only as you see Jesus, in and through your sorrows, that you will be able to say: 'It is well with my soul.' Stay with me. Let's learn how to say it together.

Hopefully, there's also some help here for those who will help others in their grief – pastors, concerned brothers or sisters in Christ, fellow church members. If we heed the commands of Romans 12, this should be all of us: 'Rejoice with those who rejoice; mourn with those who mourn' (Rom. 12:15).

If you're a Christian reading this book, then you have the privilege and the responsibility of mourning with your brothers and sisters. This is not merely a passive 'I'll sit and cry beside you,' although that's appropriate at times. To mourn with those who mourn, we must show intentional care. 'And we urge you, brothers and sisters … encourage the disheartened, help the weak, be patient with everyone' (1 Thes. 5:14). In a word, we all must encourage our fellow Christians to grieve *well*. Together, let's say: 'It is well with my soul.'

Time is on my side

What follows is a series of reflections divided into three time periods. The first set of reflections focus on 'that week,' that fateful week Megan spent in hospital before her death. These chapters all focus on the early days of uncertainty, waiting, and heartbreak. The second set of reflections focus on the immediate aftermath – from the day of Megan's death onward. The unthinkable had really happened. We had to deal with the pain, and we somehow had to carry on without Megan. These chapters are often raw and painful. The last set of reflections focus on the long-term. Our grief doesn't magically disappear three or six months on, but it does often change. These chapters aim to help you live with long-term sorrow and the general pain of life in a fallen world.

You could, I hope, dip into this book anywhere with profit, but reading these reflections in light of their context will strengthen their helpfulness. It's my sincere hope that the progression of our family's experiences will help you grieve *well* when sorrows like sea billows roll.

when sorrows like sea billows roll

Section 1: That Week

1) Inviting people in

Steve came to bring me a burrito. Because Steve is very kind, and because I have a soft place in my heart for burritos – as my increasingly soft middle section confirms – his presence on the critical care ward was encouraging. And the burrito was tasty – overflowing with flavourful chicken, bean and cheese goodness. But Steve got a whole lot more than he bargained for.

Not that long after his arrival, the doctors gave us an important update. At that point, we knew the infection-caused swelling had damaged Megan's brain. But we still didn't know the extent of the damage. We were about to find out.

Megan's mum and I were certainly going to be there for the update. I also knew my 'wingman' James would be there. But in the heat of the moment, without really thinking about it, I invited Steve into the meeting. I know Steve fairly well, but not *that* well. We're practically neighbours, we play football together semi-regularly, he's a Christian who's a part of another church yet sometimes comes along to various events our church hosts,

I once helped run an after-school Bible club with his wife. You get the picture. Steve's a friend, no doubt, but not exactly the kind of friend I expected to be in the room when the doctors told me that Megan had experienced 'catastrophic' and very likely irrecoverable brain damage.

Both the joys and sorrows of human life are better when shared. I feel this very acutely since Megan's death, and I couldn't imagine how much more difficult that season would have been without my local church. As members of the same church, we are called to 'share one another's burdens' (Gal. 6:2) while we 'rejoice with those who rejoice and mourn with those who mourn' (Rom. 12:15). I've taught these truths, our church has covenanted to carry them out, and I certainly believe them myself. And in that moment on the critical care ward, I re-discovered the sheer goodness of this Christian companionship.

I needed my brothers in that room to help me listen to and understand the doctor's diagnosis. I needed their presence to emotionally 'bear the load' of what we were hearing. I needed their counsel to help determine our next best steps. I needed them to make sure I ate well, slept, and sometimes left. We read Scripture together and prayed together; we grieved and laughed together. Steve brought a burrito, but having him (and the rest of my brothers) in that room was invaluable.

What happened by 'accident' became our modus operandi for the whole of Megan's brief time in hospital. Whoever was around when the doctors came to chat with me was invited in the room with us. Nothing was private, and no visitor was 'safe.' I would even say to the doctors about the various folks who joined us: 'Don't worry – he's basically family.' I think the doctors were a bit thrown by the size and ever-changing faces of our 'family!'

The big moments in our lives, especially our sufferings, are not 'good' to be lived alone (Gen. 2:18). Scripture proves this point again and again. Joshua and Caleb must have been encouraged by each other's presence as they stood against the other 10 spies and almost all Israel (Num. 13:30). Naomi, surely, was comforted by Ruth's commitment to her and her God in the time of their bereavement (Ruth 1:16–17). The prophet Elijah knew, by negative example, the pain one experiences when they are practically alone or appear to be so (1 Kgs. 19:10).

The apostle Paul knew better than most the need for constant Christian companionship. He's imprisoned in Philippi, and who's with him? Silas is there, and they're singing hymns together (Acts 16:24–25). He's under house arrest, presumably in Rome, and he's helped by his 'brother, co-worker, fellow soldier' and the one who took 'care of my needs' – Epaphroditus (Phil. 2:25). By the end of his ministry, after desertions and personal attacks, Paul wants companionship. He wants Mark to join him (2 Tim. 4:11).

That day on the critical care ward, as my wife lay dying, my burden was borne by my brothers. They rejoiced with my rejoicings and mourned as I mourned. I was better for their presence. This is God's design for His creatures and especially for his church. Do you believe this? When you suffer, will you invite your brothers and sisters in? Will you build patterns of living *now* that include sharing your joys and sorrows with others? Are you committed to asking for help, prayer, and biblical counsel as you face all of life's ups and downs? Your son is struggling in school, you feel overwhelmed at work and your ever-increasing remit, you're battling with a stubborn sinful habit and feel defeated – does your church family know? Have you invited them 'in the room'? Are they praying for you? Are you asking for biblically based advice and then acting on it? If we build these patterns into our church's life *now* in these 'little moments,' we'll be better prepared when 'big' suffering strikes *then*.

And Christians, will you be there and even enter into the sufferings of your brothers and sisters? Are you willing to inconvenience yourself and your family to help those who are suffering? I praise God for the countless brothers and sisters who visited me, sat with me, watched our dog, prayed for us, brought us meals, and sent me encouraging texts. You don't have to say much. Just take a burrito and be in the room.

2) The mundane

The big, traumatic moments of life can cause you to re-think your priorities. Everybody will tell you this. How you spend your money, how you use your time, how you prioritise your relationships, what you dedicate your life to – all of this is called into question when disaster strikes. Disaster had struck, and I was certainly having a re-think.

I can't remember a time I didn't enjoy sport. I like to watch it, read about it, and talk about it. I enjoy more than my share of banter with my mates! I used to even be pretty good at playing. It's even more fun now that my boys are into it – I can enjoy 'quality' time with my children *and* sport. It's a win-win! I live in north London, and there's really only one team north of the river, isn't there? Even though I live in Highbury, Tottenham Hotspur is most certainly 'the pride of north of London.' We don't get to watch many matches, but my boys and I keep up with Spurs' goings-on year in and year out. Even as I write these words, I'm wearing a Spurs shirt from a couple of years ago. The life of a Spurs (and England) supporter is a bit like masochism sometimes, I know. As Gary Lineker once said: 'Football is a simple game. Twenty-two men chase a ball for 90 minutes, and at the end, the Germans always win.'

As Megan lay in a hospital bed those last days of her life, football didn't seem quite as important. My focus was on her, our children, and the countless other things we needed to do just to get by! In one sense, football couldn't have been further from my mind. We had met with the doctors to outline a plan for Megan's care. We planned to challenge Megan's 'brain-dead' diagnosis by slowly bringing down her sedation medication while keeping her on life support. Would her brain function at all? Would she wake up? It was all up in the air. It was a difficult day filled with tumultuous emotions.

But then, suddenly, it hit me unexpectedly somewhere near the end of the day: Tottenham had played Cardiff earlier in the day. I wanted to know the result, and without thinking I reached for my phone. I remember almost instantly feeling guilty. Was I seriously going to check the result of a football match while Megan was seemingly on the verge of seeing Jesus? I was revulsed by my own inclinations and my swiftness to be interested in something so 'trivial.'

Let's be clear. From one perspective, sport (be it football, rugby, baseball, or darts) is trivial. All this fuss over a ball being kicked around a patch of grass? But from another perspective, God created mankind with the capacity to develop, play with, and enjoy creation – and sport is a reflection of this. 'God blessed them and said to them, 'Be fruitful and increase in number; fill the earth and subdue it. Rule over the fish in the sea and the birds in the sky and over every living creature that moves on the ground." (Gen. 1:28)

I don't think Adam played football in the Garden, but then I remember that rest and therefore recreation, leisure, and sport are encouraged by God. 'The Lord is my shepherd, I lack nothing. He *makes me lie down* in green pastures' (Ps. 23:1–2).

So, I had a crisis of priorities that night with my phone in my hand. What would I do? I laugh at it now, but that night I self-consciously made the choice to check the score (Spurs thrashed them 3–0). My family was grieving. We were all beyond exhaustion. The way forward wasn't anywhere near clear. Yet I am a man in need of rest; I'm a man created partially for playing with and enjoying creation. These realities didn't change during Megan's time in hospital. God made us to enjoy the mundane – dare I say, the 'trivial.' I needed to remember that. I took a few minutes and revelled in the goals that were scored, and Spurs' recent run of form and their desirable place in the table. The next day I took it a step further. As if to solidify this new-found understanding of the importance of the 'mundane' in hard times, I wore my Spurs shirt to hospital.

There's is a lesson here, I hope. If you're in the midst of grief or really any suffering, don't neglect the trivial! It's going to be hard to hear this, but don't lose a wider perspective of how God has made you as a wholistic being – spiritual and physical. Suffering has a way of prompting tunnel vision; the 'here and now' can become all-consuming. It's precisely then that you need a bit of appropriately placed triviality. How God has crafted you will determine what 'the trivial' is for you. Maybe for you it's hill-walking, picnicking, listening to music, or eating Greek souvlaki (ok, that last one is another one of mine).

Prepare yourself for suffering and bereavement in the days ahead by getting your recreation in proper perspective now. We never slide into biblical living. For a maturing Christian, recreation has its place, which means it never comes at the expense of one's responsibilities. Yes, sport can be a major time-waster (football is on the telly *every* night!). If you (or your wife!) are neglecting your other responsibilities to participate in or watch sport, then tangible repentance is needed. And this could include cutting out sport for a while. 'If your right hand causes you to sin.' Or, if you excuse irresponsibility by saying: 'I'm suffering, so I deserve a little something,' you may want to have second thoughts.

Tottenham great, Danny Blanchflower, once said: 'The game is about glory.' He's right, but maybe not in the way he meant it. To glorify God and suffer well, don't neglect the trivial. Just keep your priorities in order.

3) Radio silence

The sheer volume of texts, e-mails and proper handwritten letters I got during Megan's hospitalisation was, quite honestly, overwhelming. Our circumstances seemed to strike a chord with many. I heard reports of churches praying for us, literally, all over the world. Praise God for the worldwide body of Christ.

Rightly or wrongly, I set myself a goal to respond to every message that came through. This decision is pretty much a reflection of my personality. I'm very public about most areas of my life. Most people are naturally much more private than I am. Neither way of operating is *necessarily* wrong, although *both* can be. I can sometimes be motivated by a desire to make myself the hero in every story, and publicising my life gives me a chance to make me look good. Others can pull back into their internal bunker and in actuality fail to love others well in order to maintain their privacy.

In truth, I'm not sure it was wise for me to try and reply to *everything*. It was tiring. In fact, I asked James (and my other wing-men) to help me be disciplined with my texting. I gave myself 30 minute chunks of time that we called 'admin time.' They held me to it. I also made, under the advice of those wiser than me, the choice to have a period of 'radio silence' near the end of Megan's week in hospital. I went to a distant wing of the hospital for the whole day, which allowed me to be near Megan if things changed quickly, but not have to talk with the visitors who were daily coming to the hospital.

I suspect the thought of texting people and not being totally 'in the moment' beside Megan's bed is probably sickening to some. I get that. Some were, I think, surprised to hear from me. Some even thoughtfully said to me: 'Brad, you know you don't need to reply.' I knew, but I did anyway. I told more than one friend: 'I'm doing this for myself.' And it was true. In that moment, I had an almost constant temptation to turn inward, get sinfully discouraged, and even give up. My disciplined effort to communicate with others helped me to keep the attention off me and our trials and, instead, on God and others. As I banged out messages, I was able to remind others (but ultimately myself) what was true and right in that moment. I desperately needed that. Maybe others did too?

As strange as it sounds, my messages enjoyed an unusual clarity and focus. Scripture and helpful hymns came to mind like never before. Communicating with others, by the grace of God, afforded me unusual assurance. As the Word of God poured out of me unexpectedly, I was reminded that I really *am* a child of God (Eph. 5:1), His word really *is* true, and 'behind a frowning providence there [*really*] is a smiling face.' All of these things I have long professed to believe. And I came to find that in a moment of trial, I really believed them! Praise God!

It's worth saying that there are drawbacks to being so public about everything. I only came to see this, I think, months later. Think about yourself for a moment. Are you the kind that 'shares' most everything from your life? Or do you keep the 'cards pretty close to your chest'? Who you are and how you normally function will probably only be heightened in times of trial and bereavement.

I've heard Mark Dever say a number of times: 'The Christian life is always personal, but it's never private.' Have you unhelpfully kept your life in the shadows? Or, at least, have you failed to be open about your struggles with sin, things that are hard for you or are bringing you joy? Others share everything about everything, and maybe need to draw back for various reasons. It may be boasting or it may be searching for the approval of others. Some of us need to be slower to speak and quicker to listen. If we are going to grieve well, we must both speak and be quiet. We must share our lives with others and yet be discerning in how we do it.

Will you take steps to grow in sharing information about your life with your brothers and sisters now, so that you're prepared for the grief that will one day come?

when sorrows like sea billows roll

4) Conflict dealt with leads to critical care comfort

Recently, the children and I were recounting some of the bigger arguments Megan and I had. Like all married couples, we had our share. As we recalled a few, we had a good laugh, even though at the time those arguments were very painful. I'm sure Megan would enjoy this, and to be honest the light-hearted reminiscing was good for us.

One fight stands out. Megan and I had a 'knock down drag out' row over whether or not we should upgrade to a video doorbell. Our old doorbell had been dead for a few months – perhaps due to my lingering irresponsibility. We'd needed a doorbell for awhile. Now Megan had done the research like she always did. She'd price compared. She'd read reviews. And she came to a conclusion. I, on the other hand, hadn't done any research. I hadn't priced a thing, let alone looked at doorbells online. But she was determined we needed this certain doorbell, and I wasn't having it.

We were on our way to church when the argument began. Why do arguments so often begin just when you're on the way to church? Tempers flared, accusations were made. I surely sinned against Megan, and she against me. Maybe I was unkind or inconsiderate of her and all the work she'd done? (I definitely was.) Maybe she lashed out at me in anger and said something derogatory? (She definitely did.)

Of course, all of this happened in front of the children. The specifics are a little hazy, but I do remember a lingering hostility as we got to church. The air of resentment followed us in. Does this sound like your family? Your marriage? 'Little' issues so easily become big issues. A life pattern of annoyances and habits boil over into sinful displays. God isn't glorified, and it's not good for us. It's not an overstatement to say that the 'ships' of many marriages have crashed on the 'rocks' of such arguments.

As I reflect back on Megan's last week in the run up to her death, one omission looms large, and I actually said this to people at the time: I could think of no unresolved conflict between us. None. That week was devoid of hurt feelings, animosity, or uncertainty about whether we were 'at peace.' Megan and I had our fair share of arguments, annoyances, and marital grievances. Every marriage does. There's a reason why Megan and I, when doing marriage prep with couples, discuss conflict resolution during three of the six sessions. No, ours was not a perfect marriage, but it was – normally, by the close of every day – a reconciled marriage.

The Bible says so much about conflict. So many Christians don't realise this or have never been trained to solve conflict God's way. The Bible, ever since Eden, assumes conflict. Think over the sweep of biblical history – God's people are never without quarrels. Even in the presence of Jesus, the disciples argued! Paul and Barnabas (Mr. 'encouragement' himself!) were forced to go their separate ways after a conflict about the makeup of their ministry team. Paul experienced conflict, and a number of his letters address interpersonal conflict in the churches that were often spurred on by theological issues.

Do I really need to convince you that your marriage, your family, your church are no different? This book isn't a full biblical treatment on conflict – where it comes from, how it affects us, and how it is to be resolved. As an entry-level look at the topic, I can do no better than recommend *Resolving Everyday Conflict* by Ken Sande and Kevin Johnson. If you want to think about conflict more deeply, pick up Ken Sande's *The Peacemaker* or any resources from Peacemaker Ministries.

I do however want to quickly mention and draw out their principles from three passages that defined our approach to marital conflict. In the Sermon on the Mount, Jesus establishes the basic principle: go and work through conflict, especially where there's sin between you and a brother or sister. 'Therefore, if you are offering your gift at the altar and there remember that your brother or sister has something against you, leave your gift there in front of the altar. First go and be reconciled to them; then come and offer your gift' (Mt. 5:23–24).

Our worship of God is hindered and ought to be 'put on hold' in order to be reconciled with our spouse, our children, our colleagues, etc. Obviously, some conflicts can't be easily resolved. But where sin has crept into our relationships, Jesus charges us to go and address it: 'If your brother or sister sins, go and point out their fault, just between the two of you. If they listen to you, you have won them over' (Mt. 18:15).

Megan and I regularly approached each other in this way. She lovingly confronted me, and I lovingly confronted her. Obviously, this must be done in the context of first 'removing the plank from my own eye.' Granted, this is not an easy step, but it's essential to all conflict resolution. Then Megan and I would, inevitably, come to a point where one or both of us would have to ask for each other's forgiveness. In Christ, we've been forgiven so much, so we have a responsibility to forgive 'Bear with each other and forgive one another if any of you has a grievance against someone. Forgive as the Lord forgave you' (Col. 3:13). You've heard these verses countless times. But do you act on them regularly, even daily?

Here's the point: how you deal with conflict today will shape the pain you experience upon the death of a loved one. I'm *not* saying resolving conflict will leave you pain-free on the day of your husband's death. Far from it! Jesus wept at Lazarus' tomb, and he didn't have one inkling of an unresolved conflict with Lazarus, Mary or Martha! Think about it. How many people's grief is compounded by the fact that they never really settled things with dad? Dealing with conflict well in your family, amongst your church, and in your wider relationships *today* will bring you comfort in times of bereavement.

We reap what we sow (Gal. 6:7), so let's all take concrete steps to resolve conflict and deal with interpersonal sin today. 'If it is possible, as far as it depends on you, live at peace with everyone' (Rom. 12:18).

Our marriage was littered with routine conflict, but the critical care ward that week, by the grace of God, wasn't filled with remorse, hurt feelings and relational coldness. Praise God.

When Megan died, we hadn't yet made a final decision on the video doorbell. So, just to tell you how the argument finally ended, about a month after she died, I bought the precise video doorbell that she'd wanted. She was right after all. It's perfect.

when sorrows like sea billows roll

...rrection changes everything

Jesus is alive. It's impossible to overstate the ramifications of this reality. He *really* died, and, yes, he *really* rose again. This changes everything. For most Christians, this can seem like a distant truth. We affirm it, but we mostly think of it as a historical event, something that happened 2000 years ago. We're glad Jesus walked out of Joseph's tomb, but what direct relevance does it have to my screaming toddler? The looming deadline at work? The persistent cold that continues to plague me? Or the death of a dear wife, mother, sister, daughter and friend?

The resurrection indirectly has something to say into all of these situations. But as one day gave way to another and Megan's health deteriorated, the resurrection's significance for my family and me became clear. The resurrection of Jesus gave us all real, abiding hope. The resurrection changes everything.

Famously, the Apostle Paul describes Christians as those who 'don't grieve like the rest of mankind, who have no hope' (1 Thes. 4:13). I've preached at enough funerals to see this first hand. There is a marked difference between Christian grieving and non-Christian grieving. Both grieve, but for the Christian,

below the sadness and the pain, there is a deep undercurrent of certainty, of joy, of hope. For the wider world, there is great loss and lots of unanswered questions.

Why do Christians grieve with hope? Paul explains,

> For we believe that Jesus died and rose again, and so we believe that God will bring with Jesus those who have fallen asleep in him … For the Lord himself will come down from heaven, with a loud command, with the voice of the archangel and with the trumpet call of God, and the dead in Christ will rise first (vv14, 16).

In the face of death, Christians are hopeful because Jesus himself died and rose again. Death is an absolute and universal certainty. Nobody has come back from it and stayed alive indefinitely. Nobody, except for Jesus. He's still at it right now. And he will come back again at the 'trumpet call of God.' On that day, as Paul says, those who died in Christ will rise again. Jesus' resurrection ensures his return and the raising of all those who've 'died awaiting the promise.' It will happen. We can count on it. This changes how we view and respond to death.

As Megan's life hung in the balance, Jesus' invincible life took on fresh, personal significance. We were all so devastated, and we had a lot of unanswered questions: How could this happen to Megan? And so quickly? How could I and the seven children possibly carry on without a woman we loved so dearly and depended on for so much? What would it be like to never taste her homemade cinnamon buns again? These questions just scratch the surface.

But amidst all these unanswered questions, we had firm and sure answers to the questions that mattered most: do sin and death ultimately win? Is there any life beyond the grave?

Death is miserable and heart-breaking. And yet, Jesus is alive. We *do* lose, but not forever. Sin and death seem to have the final say on countless critical care wards, but they don't. For the elect, Jesus purchased justification and grants his now forever-resilient life. We knew with certainty: as surely as Jesus rose, Megan will rise again. I could look at her failing body ravaged by infection, and I knew, like Jesus and because of Jesus, Megan would rise again to life one day.

This certain hope doesn't negate the pain. It didn't for me, our family or our church. Death's sting is ultimately removed (1 Cor. 15:55), but it still packs quite a punch. Jesus himself experienced this. He knew he would raise Lazarus from the dead only moments later, yet he wept at Lazarus' tomb (Jn. 11:35). The pain remains, but it is tempered with a glorious hope.

I want to close this reflection with a couple of encouragements. First, study the resurrection itself. Read the explicit Old Testament promises[3] and then notice the ever-present foreshadowings. As you do, marvel.

Second, read the Gospel (that is, eyewitness!) accounts and be thrilled. Reflect on 1 Corinthians 15 and the significance of this resurrection – Paul doesn't let you take the resurrection lightly! And, of course, investigate the nascent church's reaction

---

3   For example, see: Job 19:26; Psalm 16:10, 17:15; Isaiah 25:8, 26:19; Hosea 6:2, 13:14

to the resurrection throughout the book of Acts. Didn't the resurrection change everything for the Twelve? Why wouldn't it for us, too?

Third, you'll profit from learning more about the veracity of the resurrection. Few things in all the world are more certain.[4]

Fourth and finally, delight in the 'stamp of approval' the resurrection places on the atoning work of Christ and the Christian's sure future with Him. If Jesus wasn't raised, we have nothing. Truly.

> And if Christ has not been raised, your faith is futile; you are still in your sins. Then those also who have fallen asleep in Christ are lost. If only for this life we have hope in Christ, we are of all people most to be pitied (1 Cor. 15:17–19).

In the face of Megan's imminent death, we knew we were not a piteous people. We knew our faith was not futile. Jesus is alive, and the hope of the resurrection grew up afresh in our hearts and minds.

---

4   A few helpful resources: *Is It True?: the Resurrection of Jesus* by Brian Edwards, *The Case For the Resurrection of Jesus* by Gary Habermas and Michael Lincona, and *Raised with Christ: How the Resurrection Changes Everything* by Adrian Warnock.

6) He will provide for me and turn this to my good

Adrian's handwriting was hard to read. But the letter he sent me when Megan wound up in the hospital hit the nail on the head. He didn't tell me anything that insightful; in fact, what he told me wasn't even original to him. Over two pages, Adrian simply scribbled to us nearly 500-year-old words from two men in south Germany. Those two men absolutely hit the nail on the head.

Zacharias Ursinus and Caspar Olevianus wrote The Heidelberg Catechism. The catechism, in case you're not familiar with it, is a series of questions and related biblical answers. It's an absolute treasure. It was written to pass down truth, no doubt, but it was also written to comfort the people of God - those who are safe in Jesus despite ongoing sin and ever-present trials. A number of years ago, we worked through the Catechism together as a church. We've read and studied it as a family.

But Adrian brought it to mind at just the right time. What exactly do I mean? Consider Heidelberg Catechism question 26.

Q: What do you believe when you say: I believe in God the Father almighty, Creator of heaven and earth?

On the surface, this seems like an innocuous question that needs little more than a simple theological answer. You expect something merely descriptive. But instead, the answer teaches you and comforts you. It makes you smile and encourages your heart. Ursinus and Olevianus were astute theologians with a warm, loving, and pastoral heart. Listen to the corresponding answer to the question above – learn it and let it comfort you.

Q: What do you believe when you say: I believe in God the Father almighty, Creator of heaven and earth?
A: That the eternal Father of our Lord Jesus Christ, who out of nothing created heaven and earth and all that is in them, and who still upholds and governs them by his eternal counsel and providence, is, for the sake of Christ his Son, my God and my Father. In him I trust so completely as to have no doubt that he will provide me with all things necessary for body and soul, and will also turn to my good whatever adversity he sends me in this life of sorrow. He is able to do so as almighty God, and willing also as a faithful Father.

Maybe read that again, but slowly. Notice three things:

Firstly, this Almighty God, the creator and governor of all is, due to Jesus, *my* God and *my* Father. To know that this heavenly being is not some cold, distant deity, but my God and my Father changes the complexion of the most minute details of my life. As Megan was dying and the children and I stared down the

38

barrel of life without her, my loving Father willed it to be so. He knows best, and He loves me.

Secondly, we can and should actively trust him to the degree that, whatever may come, we can be completely certain he will work it for our good. We had no idea how this could practically be the case, but we knew it to be true. Eventually, and perhaps only in eternity, will we know the 'good' that this trial will bear for my family and others. But He will work this for good – he is almighty God and faithful Father.

Finally, Ursinus and Olevianus recognise a critical reality that we felt all too keenly: this life is a life of sorrow. Isn't it? If you don't know this to be true, you haven't lived long enough. Ask anyone on a critical care ward, ask my family and church family, ask those spending their last days in a care home – all of them will tell you the same. It's true the world over - for the 1 percent and the other 99 percent, in the West as much as elsewhere. This life is full of joys, but it is a life of sorrow.

Yet despite the sorrow, Christians can take great heart. Our loving and faithful Father is working out his will, and He will turn whatever our circumstances to our ultimate good (Rom. 8:28–29). As the catechism implies, he will be with us.

> When you pass through the waters, I will be with you; and when you pass through the rivers, they will not sweep over you. When you walk through the fire, you will not be burned; the flames will not set you ablaze (Is. 43:2).

As I write this months later, I am already tasting something of the 'good' this catastrophe has brought about, but I haven't yet seen all my loving Father has planned. It still hurts, but He is with me. He really is – day by day, moment by moment.

If you're at all shaky on this truth, now is the time to hammer out your understanding of God's sovereignty. Study Scripture, talk with your elders, read a book like *Big God* by Orlando Saer. You could do worse than study the Heidelberg Catechism and other rich reformed confessions and catechisms. Kevin DeYoung has written an excellent book on the Heidelberg Catechism called *The Good News We Almost Forgot*. Check it out. You don't want to have to figure these things out in the fire. Instead, prepare yourself now. It is possible because of our loving and faithful Father. Thanks for the reminder, Adrian.

7) Fuller gospel partnership

The evangelical church in the UK is small relative to our population, certainly compared to countries like the United States or Korea. Because we are small, pastors and churches tend to recognise we need each other. We 'partner together' for all sorts of good endeavours. We pray together, evangelise together, train pastors together, etc. Partnership in the gospel means our small-ish church can gain from the resources of other churches, and hopefully we can share what God has given to us.

All this is good and well. We praise God for it.

I have just returned from the FIEC (Fellowship of Independent Evangelical Churches) leaders conference. It was a joyful and encouraging time as church leaders from all over the UK gathered for sound Bible teaching, prayer, fellowship and fun. We are together seeking to strengthen Jesus' church and reach Britain with the gospel. We really are, as the cliched line goes 'better together.' This conference was one small demonstration of that partnership.

Since Megan died, I have seen with crystal clarity another aspect of our gospel partnership that we rarely think about and almost never discuss. Our churches partner together in suffering.

Here's something of how it works. An individual Christian or family suffers. Quickly, his church rallies round with all sorts of help – practical, spiritual, emotional, etc. Obviously, the greater the suffering, the greater the help needed. It's here our wider partnership is hopefully revealed. Where greater help is needed, other churches step in to fill the gap. Not only that, but other churches also stand with that family or their church to share in their grief and bear their burden.

We had a meal provided every night for over three months. There were a few repeats in there, but that was largely distinct families preparing the food. Our church, at the time, only had 40 members. These saints carried more than their fair share, but those meals often came from other churches. To be fair, a few unbelieving neighbours also got in on the act, but praise God for gospel partnership.

That was just the beginning. Across our family of churches and beyond, so many were praying for us. Other local pastors checked in on our elders and our church members. Hours and hours of childcare were provided. Christians cried together and, when appropriate, laughed together at God's kind providences in the midst of trial.

This is gospel partnership at its richest and rawest. In late December and early January, gospel-preaching churches across the north of London partnered together in suffering. Our church gained from the resources of other churches, and hopefully we shared what God has given to us.

I couldn't convey to people the network of support we'd had. I'm not sure people believed me, to be honest. For instance, it seems like we were in the GP's surgery quite a lot over those days. After Megan's infection was clearly delineated and the public health authorities got involved, all of the children and I had to have 10 days of intense antibiotics – the kind of antibiotics that upset your tummy! Point being, on each visit, the GP was brilliant about asking after us. Each time I was there, especially if it was a different doctor, they'd take a few minutes to ask me how we were doing. I then tried to explain: 'See, I'm a Christian pastor (yes, like a vicar), and our church is amazing. And the wider network of help we've had has been mind-blowing. We are doing about as well as one could expect at a time like this.' I meant it. They nodded and smiled, but I think they were sceptical.

We saw Philippians 1:27 acted out in real time:

> Whatever happens, conduct yourselves in a manner worthy of the gospel of Christ. Then, whether I come and see you or only hear about you in my absence, I will know that you stand firm in the one Spirit, striving together as one for the faith of the gospel. For it has been granted to you on behalf of Christ not only to believe in him, but also to suffer for him'

We have a great gospel – we've been saved by the grace of God through the finished work of Jesus. These Christians, these churches, 'conducted themselves in a manner worthy of the gospel.' Their behaviour reflected and adorned the gospel we proclaim. It was beautiful and fitting. We all stood firm in one Spirit and strove together through this trial.

Paul recognises that the Philippians have and will suffer in their gospel unity. I'm guessing persecution and

43

imprisonment were more the suffering Paul had in mind, but certainly Christians are to suffer together through all sorts of trials, including bereavement. And this shared suffering is gospel partnership. I reckon our brothers and sisters in the underground churches of North Korea know something of this partnership in ways we will never grasp.

Ironically, it can be through this gospel partnership that our evangelistic efforts really take off. After all, Jesus says, the world will know we are his by our love for one another (Jn. 13:35). Mission weeks, evangelistic meetings, and one-to-ones are good, but as we suffer together, our witness gains credibility and is beautifully adorned. We declare the love of God in Christ through his shed blood on the cross, and we demonstrate something of it though our care for our suffering brothers and sisters. The world sees this and is astounded, and sometimes a hearing is gained. Maybe this partnership in suffering and its effect upon the gospel's advance is one reason James was able to say: 'Consider it pure joy, my brothers and sisters, whenever you face trials of many kinds' (1:2). Trials produce perseverance, yes; but they can also further the gospel. In the secularising West (and especially in the UK) where more direct persecution looms on the horizon, maybe a more developed understanding of gospel partnership is needed.

8) Suffering leads to encouragement?

Job has long been one of my favourite books of the Bible. I love that throughout the book the reader knows more than Job himself. We have the inside perspective that radically affects our understanding. Because we see from God's 'point of view,' we get to watch Job, initially, suffer well, and the reader knows he suffers due to no fault of his own. If only we might respond to suffering that well!

As we read on through this fuller perspective, we get to question (and rubbish) most of Job's friends' counsel, and we get to watch Job struggle as time passes. Finally, we get a ringside seat for Job's encounters with Elihu and ultimately God himself. As Job comes to know God in a profoundly richer way, we can too. As Job is silenced before the holiness of God, so should we be silenced before the holiness of God.

The point of the book of Job is not to answer the questions we ask, questions like 'Why do bad things happen to good people?' Instead, Job answers the questions we *should* be asking, like 'Just how wise *is* God?' We'll come back to Job again at another time. For the moment, I draw our attention to Job to raise one illustrative point: his suffering encourages us. In other words, it benefits us to look in on Job's suffering from outside.

Don't hear me wrong. Of course no one reads Job and celebrates Job's misfortune. To put it bluntly, you can profit from seeing others suffer. Christians especially profit from seeing older brothers and sisters suffer *well*.

Don Carson has said on a number of occasions, 'So much of the Christian life is caught as much as taught.' His point: Christian disciples are formed as much by observation as by Bible teaching. The Lord Jesus himself seemed to operate on this basis: 'Jesus went up on a mountainside and called to him those he wanted, and they came to him. He appointed twelve *that they might be with him* and that he might send them out to preach' (Mk. 3:13–14, italics mine).

Jesus would teach the Twelve, and we have record of it. But just as important, we know the Twelve were with him for something like three years. Lessons in the school of humility, obedience, and joyful service to be sure! From Jesus the Twelve also learned how to suffer well. Years later, Peter recounts what he learned to his readers:

> To this you were called, because Christ suffered for you, leaving you an example, that you should follow in his steps.
> He committed no sin, and no deceit was found in his mouth.' When they hurled their insults at him, he did not retaliate; when he suffered, he made no threats. Instead, he entrusted himself to him who judges justly (1 Pet. 2:21–23).

Jesus suffered well, and Peter had 'caught' it.

In the past several months, it has become clear how much was 'caught' during our suffering. By the grace of God, even as we grieved, we heard from various friends just how much they'd grown through our difficult time. My first response, then and now, is to praise God. What a remarkable thing that God can bring good in the lives of His children through our trials.

One friend from church wrote to me three days before Megan died. She wanted to encourage me in the midst of that terrible week. Here's what she said:

> In the midst of your chaos and pain, I wanted to share with you a bit of encouragement – the blessing I'm getting to see outside the doors of the Critical Care Unit.
>
> I am seeing an outpouring of love from around the globe, for you, Megan, your family, and your church. I'm seeing donations, special prayer groups, and tears from almost a dozen different nations. I'm seeing the Church abroad minister to the local church here in London in a way that truly honours the Lord.
>
> I am seeing fellow servants from around London and the whole UK rally together to support the work here, to check what needs your family and our congregation have right now, or may have in the future.
>
> And I am seeing the believers at St Giles grow in faith and love for each other in a way that is immensely encouraging. I am seeing them minister in new ways and share the gospel with a new boldness and renewed vigour. I am hearing new believers ask hard questions, and older brothers and sisters reply with hard truths, and then pray together to wrestle through the acceptance of those truths.

As you wrote this morning, man was never meant to function alone. The believer was never meant to worship and serve alone. And this congregation is showing why, and how, the local body is meant to live together. I have watched as dozens of offers were extended for your family's childcare, meals, housing, and travel. And when those needs were met for the time being, the offers were extended beyond. Friends have babysat so others could go visit Megan, or even just rest and reflect. Meals have been swapped. Rides have been shared. Friends have helped with menial tasks and household chores to encourage friends. Your congregation loves you and Megan, and they share in your pain. And I've watched as the love and care extended to you has reached further and comforted each other. Tired hands have reached out to lift others' tearful faces. 2 Thessalonians 1:3-4 says, 'We ought always to thank God for you, brothers and sisters, and rightly so, because your faith is growing more and more, and the love all of you have for one another is increasing. Therefore, among God's churches we boast about your perseverance and faith in all the persecutions and trials you are enduring.'

And I have seen this. I have been personally blessed by receiving this love and by seeing this love.

Brad, your view right now is a dark one. Would it be a stretch to say that inside that ward, you are walking in the valley of the shadow of death? But from out here, outside those hospital walls, it is not without sorrow, but it is a beautiful sight.

That note moved me then as it does now. Apparently, people were looking in on my family, our church family and our local friends, and God was teaching them both through our circumstances and by our responses. What a wonder!

I wonder who you have seen suffer well. Maybe it was a parent, a pastor, or the church you grew up in? They were beaten down but not destroyed. The Lord sustained them. You saw ... and fruit was borne in your life! Maybe stop and praise God for that person or that church. I praise God for Job and his suffering. Without it, I wouldn't know God as well. I'm guessing Job didn't have that in mind as he went through his trials.

when sorrows like sea billows roll

9) The end of history

Megan's health declined so quickly and so violently that I didn't feel like I even had time to process what was happening and what it all meant. I'm pretty sure others felt the same. We were overwhelmed by all of it. How could we not be? On the 23rd of December, Megan and I went with friends to see Handel's *Messiah* at the Royal Albert Hall. She had headaches that night, but we thought little of it. Six days later, Megan was unconscious. A week after that, she was dead.

Traumatic situations are dizzying and disorienting. I'm sure many reading this will relate. It feels like you're on a high speed train whizzing across the Kent countryside. Life is going on outside the window, but you're unaware of so much.

I praise God that our family and friends were on that 'high speed train' with us. But more importantly, I'm glad we knew where the 'train' was going and *why* it was going there.

What do I mean? We knew God's goal for all human history. To state it more personally, we knew that our loving Father was sovereignly directing this 'train' of Megan's illness and death, and that he had a good agenda in doing so. An agenda that we can know.

When a loved one suffers and dies, everyone has questions. One question, though, often dominates: 'why?' Why is this happening to me, to her, to our family? It can be infuriating not to know 'why.' It destroys people and families. Rarely does the Lord offer clear answers. Why that car crash? Why this tummy bug? Why didn't I get that promotion? Why can't we have children? We want to know specifics, but God rarely gives them. 'The secret things belong to the Lord our God, but the things revealed belong to us and to our children forever, that we may follow all the words of this law' (Deut. 29:29). But we *can* know what God has told us. God *has* given insight into why everything happens – both life's pleasures and life's pains. And knowing this agenda is crucial.

So what is God's agenda in all of history? Enter Paul's letter to the Ephesians. In Ephesians, God's purposes are helpfully described. Let's survey the data.

Data Point 1: 'He made known to us the mystery of his will according to his good pleasure, which he purposed in Christ, to be put into effect when the times reach their fulfilment – to bring unity to all things in heaven and on earth under Christ' (Eph. 1:9–10).

God's will is to, at just the right moment, bring all things under the Lordship of Jesus Christ. I'd argue that, in the context of Ephesians 1, this will is described as God's purpose or end in saving sinners, but this purpose is more comprehensive than just the salvation of sinners. This is God's grand agenda in and through all history – creation, fall, and redemption until the return of Christ. God's agenda is the exaltation of God the Son over all things forever!

Data point 2: 'His intent [God's] was that now, through the church, the manifold wisdom of God should be made known to the rulers and authorities in the heavenly realms' (Eph. 3:10).

God's purpose is that the church might display his wisdom for all heaven and earth to see. Can you piece these two data points together? God has created this world and overseen its plunge into sin. He has promised Israel a redemption through the Messiah, and then orchestrated this redemption through the incarnation and atoning death and resurrection of his Son. Finally, he has built his church and seen this gospel go out (and everything else in between) so that Jesus might be Lord and God's wisdom might be on display! What a God! What an agenda! What a salvation!

Now, let's join the dots. God's agenda for history includes even the details of our lives. That means that our suffering is a small yet significant piece of God working out his good plan. God is up to bigger things than I can even imagine. He is intricately pulling together an incomprehensible matrix of people and circumstances. Imagine the details that must be in the mind of God!

In my best moments, I reminded myself that through Megan's death the Lord is doing more than just taking her home to be with himself and away from us. He is also building his church, furthering his gospel, bringing all things under Christ's Lordship, causing His untold wisdom to be made manifest in His church. I know that much, and, well, that is enough.

How amazing is what we *do* know? Isn't it good that God knows what he's doing and why he's doing it?

The train was flying over the Kent countryside at a blistering and unsettling pace. We all felt it. There was so much we didn't know. But we knew who was conducting the train and to *what end*. God's purposes do not fail. There are no 'blips' in his agenda. He was and is bringing all things under Christ's rule that his wisdom might be made known in the church. Knowing this guards you against sinful worry and fear. It gives you daily purpose and meaningful work to do ('I can get the children to school today and do the ironing – that's good'). It grows you in the fear of God (He, actually, has all this in hand? Yes, he does). It gives you hope, and this hope helps you endure. 'We remember before our God and Father ... your *endurance* **inspired by hope in our Lord Jesus Christ**' (1 Thes. 1:3, italics and bold mine).

Are the overarching purposes of God clear in your mind? Having a clear, settled answer to this question will transform your suffering.

If you want a resource other than Scripture to help you think these things through more deeply, John Piper's reprint and commentary of a Jonathan Edwards treatise entitled *God's Passion For His Own Glory* is a great place to go. No matter what your future holds, Christian, you will be better prepared if you have a clearer view of God and his eternal purposes. The 'blur' of life is still there, but the little bits of focus are immensely helpful!

10) Music and hard times

I have a confession to make.

During the week of Megan's death, I fell into a strange routine. Every night, if I was leaving hospital on my own, I would kiss Megan good-bye, put my earbuds in and listen to the exact same song. Every night. No exceptions.

The song? 'I Heard It through the Grapevine' – no, not the Marvin Gaye version, the Creedence Clearwater Revival version. If you've never listened to it, go and do that now.

Now there's a back story to this unusual musical choice. I had been on what I like to call a musical 'kick.' In particular, I'd been listening to a healthy amount of 1970's rock. I found myself so disillusioned with modern rock music that I had determined to go 'back to the sources' – or so I thought.

So as the year wound down, I'd been listening to a lot of CCR, the Allman Brothers and Fleetwood Mac. That explains 'I Heard It through the Grapevine.' Picture me: earbuds in, enjoying all 11 minutes and 4 seconds of this slice of rock goodness. It's a simple but effective song! I tried to get from the critical care unit to my front door before the song ended, and I may have possibly done an air guitar on the Underground once or twice. Surely no one saw, but if they did, well, it's the Underground. They've seen stranger!

Why take so much time to explain this weird routine? Here's why: music was a great source of joy for me (and my family) at that time. I mean, obviously, that was an incredibly painful series of weeks and months. But that song made my toes tap, and it made my load seem just a little bit lighter.

And it wasn't just that one song. There's a wide array of music that's now forever tied to that time for me. And all of it, in one way or another, blessed me. Which means I was enjoying music as God intended. So how do we use music well, especially in dark times?

First, we need to recognise what a gift music is. It didn't take long before man, created in the image of God, went on to create music. Music is first formally mentioned in scripture in Genesis 4:21. 'His brother's name was Jubal; he was the father of all who play stringed instruments and pipes.' I'm guessing it would have been fun to be there listening to Jubal. We know so little about his actual music, but it had to have been aesthetically pleasing! I'm thinking scripture wouldn't have made record of Jubal's music if it was rubbish.

It's simply fun to listen to good music – from Mozart to Thelonious Monk. And amidst the ever-increasing pressure and intensity of our circumstances, we needed something to enjoy. The steady stream of visitors, the conversations with the doctors, the uncertainty about Megan's life and last days, all of this was excruciating. Yet music was uplifting, diverting and fun – as it should be.

Second, during tough times we realise how much we've learned from music throughout the years. Good theology set to good music can be a wonderful educational tool. That's why the apostle Paul encouraged the use of music in the church: 'Let the message of Christ dwell among you richly as you teach and admonish one another with all wisdom *through* psalms, hymns, and songs from the Spirit, singing to God with gratitude in your hearts' (Col. 3:16, italics mine). Music has the uncanny ability to get stuck in our heads, and if it's communicating truth (about God, salvation through Jesus, or the Christian's hope of heaven), music can direct our hearts and minds 'above, where Christ is' (Col. 3:1). During the duration of Megan's time in hospital, I was almost constantly playing at home the *Together for the Gospel Live* albums – collections of hymns old and new accompanied by only a piano and the voices of thousands. I was being taught so much rich theology, even if my children were growing sick of hearing the same songs over and over!

While I sat next to Megan's hospital bed, music kept coming to mind. As you might have guessed, 'It Is Well With My Soul' offered a constant source of encouragement. What a declaration:

> When peace like a river attendeth my way
> when sorrows like sea billows roll,
> whatever my lot, thou has taught me to say:
> it is well, it is well with my soul.

As I've said already, I knew something of 'sea billows,' and God was teaching me to say 'it is well.'

After Megan died, we wanted to make sure her funeral featured some good, Christ-exalting music. We worked hard to select easy-to-sing songs that both captured our hope and held significance for our family and church.

Christians singing can be a tremendous witness to lost listeners. One of the teaching assistants at my children's primary school lives just down from our church building. She's told me more than once that she loves it when her windows are open in the summer months because she can listen to St Giles' singing.

Now I pray that the truth she hears might bear fruit in her life! It wouldn't be the first time that's happened in church history. 'About midnight Paul and Silas were praying and singing hymns to God, and the other prisoners were listening to them' (Acts 16:25) We don't know the direct impact of Paul and Silas' singing on the other prisoners, but we do know the jailer (who may have heard them as he was falling asleep!) was profoundly affected. The singing at Megan's funeral gave God's people a chance to glorify our God of grace, and I pray it drove home gospel truths to the unbelievers who were present.

Let me mention one final use of music. Music allows us the opportunity in hard times to simply praise God. Aren't many of the psalms based precisely on this principle? The psalmists (David especially) knew trials and pain. Examples abound, but here's one: 'The Lord is my strength and my shield; my heart trusts in him, and he helps me. My heart leaps for joy, and with my song I praise him' (Ps. 28:7). Praise amidst trials – God deserves it, and it's right for us to give it.

11) I'll drop everything

In the busyness of Megan's time in hospital, I had a rule for myself. The rule? No matter what was happening, who I was with, or who I was talking to, I would drop everything to answer my children's phone calls. The rule had one exception (of which my children were aware). Because we often waited so intently for an update from the doctors, I wouldn't answer the phone if I was chatting with a doctor. A pretty simple rule, but I think it did reap fruit at the time, and I pray it continues to reap fruit in the future.

This rule gave my children immediate access to me. We decry the invasiveness of mobile phones and social media – and for good reason! – but what a help my phone was during that time.

For just over a week my routine was usually a simple one: if I slept the night before, I'd be up for breakfast with the family and then out the door to hospital – usually meeting my 'wing man' outside the Underground station. On occasion, my children came with me in hospital, but they were usually home with extended family or other helpful friends. So, I'd be in hospital all day without them, and I wouldn't come back till well after their bed time.

I've been slowly reading *David Copperfield* at the time of writing this. I've not yet finished it, but I was struck early on by how poorly young David Copperfield is cared for around the time of his mother and her baby's untimely deaths. Dickens captures something of the deep emotion and the painful longing of that time for anybody, especially children. David (who's away at the time of his mother's death) wants consolation, affection and explanation. He gets none from his step-father (the grizzly-named Mr Murdstone); this compounds his heartache. Thankfully, the longstanding family servant Pegotty provides what David so needs. David doesn't see much of Pegotty, but most nights, she sits at the head of his bed and helps him get to sleep. Importantly, Pegotty explains the circumstances surrounding David's mum's death, which included an expression of her love for David. This is what children (but not children only!) need during times of loss, isn't it?

What Pegotty did, in explaining the circumstances surrounding David's mother's death, is so difficult. In a slightly different way, this lot fell to me late on New Year's Eve (even before my 'rule' came into effect). Earlier that day, we were told that Megan was clinically brain-dead and was almost certainly unable to live without life support. I had to, somehow, convey this reality to my six children. I mean, how do you prepare for a conversation like that? I still don't know, but as it turns out, I just kept it really simple.

When I got back home, I was eager to get unhurried time with the children (at least the five who were still awake). We sat on my bed, and I pretty much told the children what the doctors had earlier told me. Then, we cried, we laughed, we were quiet for long spells and we reminisced for I don't know how long. At the children's prompting, I opened my birthday presents. Yes, the 31st of December happens to be my birthday, and Megan had already wrapped my birthday presents a few weeks earlier, even before she started having the headaches. Her writing was on the wrapping paper! This made us laugh and cry even more. The night ended when the children and I went downstairs to pray with our gathered friends and family. What a night, and this kicked off the last week of Megan's life here on earth.

Parenting in the midst of significant tragedy is difficult, to put it very mildly. I am not sure I have a lot of wisdom to offer on the whole. So much about parenting at times like this will depend on your circumstances, your various personalities, and your family situation. And yet, in advance of tragedy, it's wise to at least have a little think about it, isn't it? I raise my 'rule' not to convince you that somehow I marvellously parented my six (and by that point seven) children through this. That's just not true. But I did try. I raise my 'rule' to offer a simple principle for parents who suffer: don't neglect your responsibility to your children. Even when life's circumstances are almost unbearable for you, train and instruct your children. This may sound cold or harsh; I'm aware of that. And yet, Ephesians 6:4 is not dependent upon our circumstances. It applies at all times and all places: 'Fathers, do not exasperate your children; instead, bring them up in the training and instruction of the Lord.'

61

How did my children handle this tragedy? As differently as each of their personalities.

It was a lot for anybody to handle, but what became immediately clear was that they needed me. None of them put it this way to me directly, but they needed explanation, and they needed teaching and interpretation. They needed me to explain what was happening (what the doctors were saying, how mummy was doing, etc). They needed to see how I was grappling with all of this – both the mourning and the rejoicing, and they saw a lot of both. They needed me to teach them and set an example for them. They were listening to me, wanting to see how God's Word explains this tragedy. And they were watching me, wanting to see a Christian response to hardship.

So the question for you is simple: are you prepared to steer your children through suffering and grief? Do you, yourself, have a theology of suffering? Have you begun, even now, to talk with these children about hard things and how Christians respond to them? You have the responsibility and the privilege of shepherding your children through life's challenges. Maybe my rule will be a help to you?

12) I can't sleep

Hospital sofas aren't comfortable. That first night though after Megan first slipped into unconsciousness, I'm not sure I would have been able to sleep even if the sofa *had* been comfortable. Our baby had just been delivered, but my wife was in a perilous state. I was overwhelmed. But there I was. I stretched out on the long, white, brick-like sofa in the critical care ward 'relatives' room and tried to sleep. But I couldn't. I even put some Fernando Ortega (very calming, peaceful, sleep-inducing music) in my ears, but to no avail. That night was the beginning of a week of intermittent and irregular sleep.

I normally don't have the slightest problem falling asleep. My bedtime routine couldn't be more routine: I read a few pages, turn my lamp off and, within minutes (sometimes seconds!) I am off to sleep. And I rarely wake up before my phone alarm chimes. Simply put, I'm a consistent and sound sleeper. Normally.

But that first night and the week that followed was something altogether different. I tried my hardest. After that first sleepless night, I came home the next morning and sought a few winks. I just couldn't. I finally capitulated and got up after lying in bed for two hours.

I tried hard to sleep every night. It wasn't that I left hospital particularly late. It wasn't that I was so burdened with responsibilities – so many were helping to carry the load. My sleeplessness was surely compounded by the fact that my older boys wanted to sleep in bed with me. I was glad for them to, and I appreciated the company. But they wriggle!

That's not really why I couldn't sleep. As I reflect back on that time though, I think I couldn't sleep because my mind just wouldn't slow down. Let's say my brain normally thinks at 60 miles per hour (some who know me well may debate even that speed!). Over the course of that week, it seemed like my brain was thinking at 125 miles per hour! I just couldn't calm down sufficiently for my tired body to switch off.

I wasn't necessarily worrying either, as you might suspect. I'm sure I worried some – about Megan, about our newborn, etc. But my mind was just running in overdrive. I was thinking about everything and making decisions very quickly. I'm not too keen on medicinal intervention to help promote sleep, but I finally gave in. During the middle of that week, I took a recommended dose of Piriton (a mild antihistamine) at bedtime, and rejoiced in the four or so hours of sleep that resulted!

Sleep is a good gift from God. Have you ever thought of sleep like that? It's a gift. We can't carry on forever. To try to survive without sleep is to spurn God's gift.

> Unless the Lord builds the house, the builders labour in vain.
> Unless the Lord watches over the city, the guards stand watch
> in vain. In vain you rise early and stay up late, toiling for food
> to eat – for he grants sleep to those he loves (Ps. 127:2).

And yet, sometimes we just can't sleep. There are all sorts of reasons why. These reasons can be physical, emotional, or spiritual. Asaph couldn't sleep perhaps for one or all of these reasons:

> When I was in distress, I sought the Lord; at night I stretched out untiring hands, and I would not be comforted. I remembered you, God, and I groaned; I meditated, and my spirit grew faint. You kept my eyes from closing; I was too troubled to speak (Ps. 77:2–4).

Sometimes, our sleeplessness can't be easily diagnosed. For reasons often only known to our Heavenly Father, he providentially withholds sleep.

How do we deal with the reality of sleeplessness? How do we cope with little or no sleep for a couple of days or longer? I realise for some, the answer may be one word: coffee. And those witty folks would have a point! Coffee may help you be physically awake and more alert. But my question goes a bit deeper. How do we prepare *spiritually* for the reality of sleeplessness? How do we think well and continue to serve the Lord when we're drowsy? Or when our bodies ache because we've not had the sleep we need?

I submit to you three brief bits of biblical counsel trialled during my string of sleepless nights. First, remember that God will give you the strength you need for what he gives you. If he withholds sleep and you have a big meeting the next day or you have five children under the age of 7 to look after, God will provide you the strength you need to persevere. He really will. He did and still does for me.

Don't forget that when you are weak (and especially when you know you're weak), God's power shines forth:

> But he said to me, 'My grace is sufficient for you, for my power is made perfect in weakness.' Therefore I will boast all the more gladly about my weaknesses, so that Christ's power may rest on me (2 Cor. 12:9).

If God keeps you from sleep on Monday night, then he will give you the resources to please him on Tuesday.

Sleeplessness makes living for Christ harder, but it doesn't make it impossible. Of course, it's just so hard to remember this when you feel exhausted! But the Lord will give you everything you need. And, of course, coffee can help too!

Second, let your sleeplessness drive you to God not away from Him. God is not like us. He never has problems sleeping because he never sleeps! Pause and think about that for a second: God is never worn out, never needs time away, and certainly isn't feeling frazzled. 'Indeed, he who watches over Israel will neither slumber nor sleep' (Ps. 121:4).

God draws from limitless inherent resources. This means when we can't sleep, we can and should cry out to him. Instead of letting a root of bitterness spring up or continually grasping at solutions for our sleep problem, take comfort that God is sufficient in himself and he is always at work for our good (Rom. 8:28–29). Even our sleeplessness is used by God to conform us to the image of Christ.

Thirdly and finally, take heart. Though you don't sleep well now, there is a day of rest coming for the people of God.

There remains, then, a Sabbath-rest for the people of God; for anyone who enters God's rest also rests from their works, just as God did from his. Let us, therefore, make every effort to enter that rest, so that no one will perish by following their example of disobedience (Heb. 4:9–11).

So persevere through sleeplessness now by faith in Jesus Christ and his imminent return. A rest awaits. Revelation heralds this rest, and it sounds sweet:

Then I heard a voice from heaven say, 'Write this: blessed are the dead who die in the Lord from now on.' 'Yes,' says the Spirit, 'they will rest from their labour, for their deeds will follow them' (Rev. 14:13).

Strangely, after Megan died, I slept very well. Mostly. Knowing that she had entered her rest allowed me to sleep. My mind slowed down. Praise God. I continue to sleep fairly well most nights.

I say 'most' because when our newborn got home from hospital my sleeplessness took on a different hue! Months on from Megan's death, I visited the family of a terminally ill man in our church. I sat with this family in the same room on the same brick-like white sofa I'd tried to sleep on during that fateful week. It still wasn't comfortable. As well as I'm sleeping now, I still don't think I could sleep on that sofa.

when sorrows like sea billows roll

13) I feel the bottom, and it is good

We all stand at the edge of a great river. It's a river that must be crossed, and there's no bridge or way round. To make matters worse, this river's deep and its current is brutal. Who can look upon this river and not be dumbfounded, even frightened? Christians have no easy 'out' from death and its terrors. They must go through the river if they are to go in at the gate and enter their heavenly rest.

John Bunyan takes this picture of death as a river (rooted in biblical imagery)[5] and powerfully embellishes it at the end of the first part of his *Pilgrim's Progress.*

They're almost home – to the place they've longed for. Just a stone's throw away, Christian and Hopeful can actually *see* the gates of the Celestial City. Yet there's a problem. Between Christian, Hopeful and those gates stands a seemingly impassable river. 'Is there no other way to the gate?' they ask.

It's a question we all ask. It's the question I was asking during Megan's last days. The pilgrims receive a firm answer: no. Until the return of Christ, there is no other way. Then Bunyan

---

5   See Exodus 14:29, Joshua 3:15-17, Psalm 66:12, Isaiah 43:2-3, and Hebrews 11:29

summarises, very simply, the experience of most Christians brought face-to-face with inescapable mortality: 'The pilgrims then, especially Christian, began to despond in their minds, and look this way and that, but no way could be found by them, by which they might escape the river.'

As we waited there on the critical care ward, we knew well the experience of these pilgrims. Megan stood within earshot of the heavenly gates, the end of her earthly pilgrimage. But first, she would have to cross the river.

The Bible uses a variety of images to help us understand death. Death is our deserved 'wages' for our sin against a holy God (Rom. 6:23). Death is our 'enemy' haunting and afflicting us until it finally catches up with us (1 Cor. 15:26). Death is our 'ruler' since Adam fell, reigning over us and always getting its way (Rom. 5:17 ff). Drawing from the Isaiah 43:2 ('When you pass through the waters, I will be with you; and when you pass through the rivers, they will not sweep over you ...'), Bunyan brings out another implied biblical metaphor: death is the ultimate 'waters' one passes through.

We could just leave the image there, but Bunyan helpfully presses the image slightly further yet still. Don't miss this. As the pilgrims stand on the edge of the river, they learn that the river isn't consistently deep. At some places, it's shallow; at other places, it's basically bottomless. The depth of the river depends on the faith of the one crossing.

Do you get Bunyan's point? If your faith in Christ is strong, the river will be more shallow, and you'll get across with less trouble. If your faith in Christ is weak, the river will be deeper and your crossing will be more painful. Your reaction to and experience of death depends on your faith in Christ. This a simple yet profound truth, and we'll return to it in a moment.

What happens in Bunyan's retelling? One of his characters struggles. As the pilgrims step out into the river, Christian sinks, and he's all but certain that he'll never make it to the Celestial City: 'I sink in deep waters; the billows go over my head ... The sorrows of death have compassed me about!' Bunyan tells us what Christian is feeling:

> And with that a great darkness and horror fell upon Christian
> ... And all the words that he spoke still tended to discover that
> he should die in that river and never obtain entrance at the
> gate.[6]

Bunyan captures the thoughts of many Christians. Death – and, more specifically, the act of dying – is almost overwhelming.

But back to Bunyan's idea of the varying depths. Of course, he is not denying the painfulness of death. Quite the opposite. This river crossing is painful even for those with a robust faith in Christ. Death is always painful. And frightening. But why? First of all, because God designed death to work this way. As Christians, we don't 'grieve as those who have no hope' (1 Thes. 4:13). But death still hurts. We do grieve. If death weren't painful, would it convey the gravity and offensiveness of our sin?

One of the most painful aspects of death is the severance. Death confronts us with a seemingly permanent separation.

---

6   *The Pilgrim's Progress* by John Bunyan in *The Works of John Bunyan*, The Banner of Truth Trust, 1991, vol 3, pg 163.

This river's current seems quite capable of sweeping us and our loved ones away forever.

Secondly, death is painful because our sin still haunts us. The threat of God's judgment hangs over us. As he flounders in the river, Christian says as much: 'If I was right [acceptable to God], he [Jesus] would now arise to help me; but for my sins he hath brought me into the snare, and hath left me.' In that climactic moment, Christian, a truly regenerate man, questions his justification and wonders whether his death is a sign of God's disapproval. That's sin crying out its final breath.

When I die, I hope to be more like Jesus than when I was born again. But this I know for certain: when I die, I will still be a sinner. And I will likely remember well the sins of my past. I may question whether my sin is just too much. Is God as merciful as he's promised to be? These are all scary and uncertain realities.

Hopeful, on the other hand, had an altogether different experience of the river. Oh, he was frightened just like his friend. He had also sought an alternative way around. But when the time came to actually cross the river, Hopeful found sure footing even as Christian sank below the billows. After stepping out into the water, he says to flailing Christian: 'Be of good cheer, my brother, I feel the bottom, and it is good.'

Step by step, Hopeful crossed the river trusting in the promises of God and remembering the never-failing love of Christ. Hopeful's faith changed his experience of death. He was truly and practically

> Convinced that neither death nor life, neither angels nor
> demons, neither the present nor the future, nor any powers,

> neither height nor depth, nor anything else in all creation, will
> be able to separate us from the love of God that is in Christ
> Jesus our Lord (Rom. 8:38–39).

Hopeful was able to say, as he stepped into the river, something like: 'You promised this God. And I am going to take you at your word. This whole dying thing is terrible, but nothing will separate me from your love. I *will* cross this river, and I *will* walk through the gates into the celestial city.'

Will you approach your death with that same sort of certainty? Will you respond to the death of a beloved spouse, child, parent or friend with similar faith? Will you find sure footing to cross this painful river?

Start preparing now. How? Learn about and remember the character and promises of God. Read your Bible, listen to the Word preached faithfully week in and week out in your local church, study good theology. You could do worse than slowly reading your way though a solid volume of systematic theology.

When you're about to die, you want to have a clear mind about God's character, Jesus' atoning work and God's promises to his people. You want to be able to recall Psalm 103:10–12 in a moment:

> He does not treat us as our sins deserve or repay us according
> to our iniquities. For as high as the heavens are above the
> earth, so great is his love for those who fear him; as far as the
> east is from the west, so far has he removed our transgressions
> from us.

You ought to expect from God the same treatment ancient Israel received: 'In your unfailing love you will lead the people you have redeemed. In your strength you will guide them to your holy dwelling' (Ex. 15:13). Death will test your resolve. Death will shine a searchlight on your faith, and it will expose the cracks. So prepare yourself for this reckoning.

Bunyan puts it so well as Hopeful reflects upon his own river crossing:

> These troubles and distresses that you go through in these waters are no sign that God hath forsaken you; but are sent to try you, whether you will call to mind that which heretofore you have received of his [God's] goodness, and live upon him in your distresses.[7]

Will you, at the point of death, call to mind what you have received? Will you 'live on him' in your distresses?

I read this bit of *Pilgrim's Progress* aloud to Megan as she unconsciously lay there in her hospital bed. I honestly don't know what she heard. But I do know that I wept – and I rejoiced. Megan's river crossing was sudden, but I'm confident she made it across. She most certainly found a firm footing. So, by the grace of God I pray, have I. Your reaction to and experience of death depends on your faith in Christ. So get to know Christ now. 'Feel the bottom' of the river *now*, so you can declare on that day: 'It *is* good.'

---

7   pg 163-164.

14) A world of love

As I sit to write this particular chapter, it's exactly two years from the day Megan died. The memories come flooding back in. It's a bittersweet day. I miss Megan, and yet I'm filled with joy for her life and our marriage. I'm also delighted to know exactly where Megan is.

Some speak of death as having 'lost' a loved one. I get what they mean, and I've spoken in the same way myself at times. But I also recognise that I haven't 'lost' Megan at all. I know *precisely* where she is. JC Ryle once said: 'I pity the man who never thinks about heaven.'[8] Ryle's right: such a man is worthy of our pity, especially if he or his loved one comes to die and he's still never thought about heaven.

At the time of Megan's death, by the grace of God, my family and I were thinking a lot about heaven. The Bible's teaching on heaven has always been a topic of rich comfort for Christians. To know that Jesus has gone on ahead and is 'preparing a place' for his people (Jn. 14:3), to know that the moment you die you will be with Jesus 'in paradise' (Lk. 23:43), to know that

---

8 Randy Alcorn, *Heaven*, Tyndale House Publishers, 2004, pg8. Alcorn draws this quote from J.C. Ryle, *Heaven*, Christian Focus Publications, 2000, pg19.

in heaven an inheritance awaits that 'will never perish, spoil or fade' (1 Pet. 1:4). These truths are such a consolation amidst the pain of death.

But what will heaven *actually* be like? Our knowledge is limited to what the Bible tells us. We know, mostly importantly, that when the Christian dies he immediately goes to be with Jesus, and this is better by far (Phil. 1:20–21; 2 Cor. 5:8). We also know that heaven, as it is at present, will give way to the new heavens and the new earth upon the return of Christ (Is. 66:22; Rev. 21:1–27). The heavens and the earth as we now know them will be reshaped to be free from sin and all its deleterious effects.

So we know what *won't* be in the New Heavens and New Earth: tears, death, mourning, crying or pain (Rev. 21:4). What a wonderful, relieving truth! We also know that God will dwell there with his people, and they will see his face (Rev. 22:3–5). God's people will reign with Him for all eternity in a new heavens and a new earth.

Question 38 in the Westminster Shorter Catechism beautifully summarises the inheritance that awaits believers:

Question: What benefits do believers receive from Christ at the resurrection?

Answer: At the resurrection, believers, being raised up in glory, shall be openly acknowledged and acquitted in the day of judgement, and made perfectly blessed in the full enjoying of God to all eternity.

Did you catch that? *Perfectly blessed*, fully enjoying God for all eternity. Thomas Boston gets it: 'All men must die, but as men's lives are very different, so their account in death is, also. To an ungodly man, death is loss, the greatest loss; but to a believer, it is gain, the greatest gain.'[9]

One person who thought a lot about heaven and its perfect blessedness is Jonathan Edwards. As Megan lay there in her hospital bed during those last few hours before entering the presence of her Lord, I read aloud to her Jonathan Edwards' sermon 'Heaven, a World of Love.' If you've not yet read this sermon, you really should.

Edwards' meditations on heaven are extremely comforting, yet stirring. He understands what will be the believers' greatest joy in heaven:

> There [in heaven], above all, we shall enjoy and dwell with God the Father, whom we have loved with all our hearts on earth; and with Jesus Christ, our beloved Saviour, who has always been to us the chief among ten thousands, and altogether lovely; and with the Holy Ghost, our sanctifier and guide, and comforter; and shall be filled with all the fulness of the Godhead forever![10]

In heaven, we shall be with and *enjoy* our triune God.

Gone are the notions of heavenly boredom! Gone are the lazy ideas of a subpar heavenly experience! You, believer, will be delighted head to toe with and in the presence of your loving Father, your Saviour the Son, and your comforter the

---

9 Thomas Boston, *The Complete Works of Thomas Boston*, Tentmaker Publications, 2002, volume 2, pg37.

10 Jonathan Edwards, *Charity and Its Fruits*, The Banner of Truth Trust, 1969, pg 332.

Holy Spirit. And this joy will be ever-increasing as you'll spend all eternity getting to know God better and better. Imagine that: ever-increasing joy! I honestly can't fathom that. But it's true. Edwards again: 'And thus in the full sunlight of the throne, enraptured with joys that are for ever increasing, and yet for ever full, they shall live and reign with God and Christ for ever and ever!'[11]

Heaven will also be a place of perfect and unalterable peace: 'In that soul where divine love reigns and is in lively exercise, nothing can cause a storm or even gather threatening clouds.'[12] He goes on: 'Oh! What tranquility will there be in such a world as this! And who can express the fulness and blessedness of this peace! What calm is this! How sweet, and holy and joyous!'[13] Perhaps you can grasp the possibility of this. But you've surely never experienced it. But you will, Christian. You, rebel adopted into this great inheritance by the grace of God, will enjoy this kind of peace. (You really should read this sermon. It's heart-lightening and mind-blowing stuff.)

But what about today? What should we think about in the bedrooms, offices, and critical care wards of our lives? Edwards helps us there as well:

> In all your ways let your eyes be fixed on Jesus, who has gone to heaven as your forerunner. Look to him. Behold his glory in heaven, that a sight of it may stir you up the more earnestly to desire to be there. Look to him in his example.

---

11 pg 353, italics mine.

12 pg 350

13 pg 351

Consider how, by patient continuance in well-doing, and by patient endurance of great suffering, he went before you to heaven. Look to him as your mediator, and trust in the atonement which he has made, entering into the holiest of all in the upper temple. Look to him as your intercessor, who for ever pleads for you before the throne of God. Look to him as your strength, that by his Spirit he may enable you to press on, and overcome every difficulty of the way. Trust in his promises of heaven to those that love and follow him, which he has confirmed by entering into heaven as the head, and representative, and Saviour of his people.[14]

Jesus is not only our ground for hope in heaven, he's also our forerunner there. Eyes that are fixed on Jesus can't help but look to and anticipate heaven.

I know where Megan is. She's with Jesus. She has been for the last two years, and her joy there will only continue to increase for all eternity. By the grace of God, I too will join them one day. JC Ryle gets it: 'Those whom you laid in the grave with many tears are in good keeping: you will yet see them again with joy. Believe it, think it, rest on it. It is all true.'[15]

---

14 pg 367

15 Randy Alcorn, Heaven, Tyndale House Publishers, 2004, pg 373. Alcorn draws the quote from J. C. Ryle, *Heaven*, Christian Focus Publications, 2000, pg84.

when sorrows like sea billows roll

15) Angry with God

I'm a Calvinist, which means I believe God is sovereign over all things. 'He does as He pleases ... No one can hold back his hand' (Dan. 4:35). God determines the day of our birth, the day of our death and every day in between. 'All the days ordained for me were written in your book before one of them came to be' (Ps. 139:16).

Therefore, though it sounds shocking, it's true to say that God took my wife from me. This might give you an apparent reason to be angry with God. That's what many do after a loved one dies. They get angry with God. They blame Him for their heartache, they question His goodness, they struggle to pray or go to church, and they generally feel frosty towards Him. That is, if they don't reject God altogether. It's what Mrs Job told Job to do: 'Curse God and die' (Job 2:9). God's sovereignty makes some people angry.

Some people would say that I have a reason or two to be angry. On the 31st December, I received word that my wife, the mother of my seven children would almost certainly die. It was supposed to be a happy day. It was New Year's Eve! It was my birthday! We'd planned to host an 'open house' that evening. Instead, I was telling my children that their mother would die – and a week later, she was gone.

From that point on, I was a single dad of seven. I had children to comfort, and some very important family decisions to make. All this carried with it the backdrop that I wasn't sure if I would be able to carry on in ministry. To be honest, it seemed unlikely. Just under two weeks later, our newborn came home to a world without his mum. And I, still grieving my wife's death, now had a newborn to look after.

God is absolutely sovereign, but *this* is where His plan had led me? And it only got harder. But my question is a simple one: should I have been angry? Should I be angry now? Think for a moment: would this have made you angry?

Let me state up front what I'm *not* trying to do. I am not trying to 'defend' God. There are many able 'defences' of God's sovereignty in suffering. One of my favourite, if you want to wrestle with this topic more, is *How Long O Lord: Reflections on Suffering and Evil* by DA Carson. Instead, I am trying to explain how I didn't fall headlong into the ditch of anger and bitterness. To be sure, there were certainly moments of anger in those early days. There still are now. But, by the grace of God, I don't think anger has generally characterised my life since Megan's death. I have been angry with God, but I haven't been an angry man. Why is that? And how can you similarly avoid it?

I want to offer three individuals who could have been angry with God, but weren't. What can we learn from them? Let's lay out the lessons before we summarise.

First, let's have another look at Job. Job's reputation and his suffering precede him. Job is described as 'blameless and upright; he feared God and shunned evil ... He was the greatest man among all the people of the East' (Job 1:1–3). And yet, his suffering almost matched his greatness. Wave after wave of messengers reported to Job that his 10 children had all died, his livestock had either died or been stolen, and a large number of his servants had been murdered. Can you imagine the emotions Job must have been feeling?

And then it got worse.

Soon after, he's covered in painful sores from head to toe. His wife then begs him to angrily curse God and die. Some might not blame her. But Job's response is unreal: 'Naked I came from my mother's womb, and naked I shall depart. The Lord gave and the Lord has taken away; may the name of the Lord be praised' (Job 1:21). And then: 'Shall we accept good from God, and not trouble?' (Job 2:10) Job humbly submits to God's sovereign will. He resigns himself to the fact that though he could get angry, it wouldn't do any good. God gives good, and God gives trouble. Whatever He decides to give is His prerogative. But God always deserves our praise. There's a lesson for us here, isn't there?

Joseph also had reasons to be angry with God. Beloved by his father but betrayed by his brothers. The pledge of pre-eminence he received by dream probably didn't seem so great from the bottom of a cistern. Sold into slavery, falsely accused of immorality and punished for it, passed over for release from prison – the list could go on.

Throughout his story we know little of Joseph's attitude toward God. But we get a few strong hints. First, when Joseph is solicited by his master's wife, you'd think Joseph might have a reason to 'live a little,' especially when you consider his difficult upbringing. And yet, he says: 'My master has with held nothing from me except you, because you are his wife. How then could I do such a wicked thing and sin against God?' (Gen. 39:9) Joseph doesn't feel bitter and therefore justified in his indulgence of sin. Not Joseph. Here we have a hint of Joseph's regard for God. A bitter man he is not.

A second telling moment comes when Joseph's brothers reappear on the scene. At that point, Joseph has both the authority and the motive to exact his revenge. And yet, here's how he responds to them: 'You intended to harm me, but God intended it for good to accomplish what is now being done, the saving of many lives' (Gen. 50:20). How is Joseph not angry? Well, Joseph sees (with hindsight, mind you) that God has good intentions behind even the worst suffering.

Lastly, consider the Lord Jesus. Where to start? Co-eternal with the Father and the Spirit, in very nature God and deserving of the highest heavenly praises. Yet the Son condescends to take on humanity. Throughout his earthly life and ministry, Jesus is questioned, mocked, and plotted against. He's essentially identified with the devil (Mk. 3:22), and treated as such. 'He was despised and rejected by mankind, a man of suffering, and familiar with pain. Like one from whom people hide their faces he was despised, and we held him in low esteem' (Is. 53:3). That would make anyone angry.

And then there's that climactic final week. Jesus is betrayed by a close friend, and then deserted by everyone. He's falsely accused, shouted down by the crowd, and unjustly condemned. He's beaten, jeered at, and then, finally, crucified. He suffers an excruciating death. Worst of all, Jesus is forsaken by God (Mk. 15:34). He's treated as the worst of sinners, bearing the wrath of God (2 Cor. 5:21; Is. 53:5).

Surely Jesus would turn on God? Surely He would rage against the sovereign will of His Father? No. 'He was oppressed and afflicted, yet he did not open his mouth; he was led like a lamb to the slaughter, and as a sheep before its shearers is silent, so he did not open his mouth' (Is. 53:7). Jesus willingly faced suffering and death. In fact, Jesus went to the cross anticipating, of all things, *joy*. 'For the joy that was set before him he endured the cross, scorning its shame' (Heb. 12:2).

Our Saviour knows untold pain. Some would say he should have been vindictive and angry. Yet He underwent severe suffering to purchase our redemption. Jesus knew that he would be raised to new life and seated at the Father's right hand, but that probably seemed a long way from the cross. Jesus saw past the suffering to the results it would accomplish. There's a lesson here for us, without a doubt.

Let's summarise. How can anyone avoid bitterness and anger in times of suffering? A cancer diagnosis, a house burgled, a child bullied, a house fire, a redundancy, a rape – these are hard providences. Anger-provoking. Some of these examples call for righteous anger, a zeal to make things right. But how can we not turn *on God* in anger? When we feel hot, wronged, disappointed, hurt, and enraged? What do we do?

Firstly, Job's submission to God directs us. God gives and God takes away. We can and must actively submit to the Lord. We might say something like: 'God, I don't like this, but I trust you. You alone are God only wise.' We move away from anger by humbly submitting

Secondly, Joseph's ability to see through the hardship challenges us. Joseph recognises, with hindsight, the good that hard providences bring. We must be patient in suffering, and wait to see the good fruit. Anger toward God misses God's good, overarching plan. Our tempers can be defused by fiercely waiting. 'Everyone should be quick to listen, slow to speak and slow to become angry' (Jas. 1:18–19). Slowing down really can help.

Thirdly, Jesus helps us most. Of course He does. Our Saviour suffered more than any of us ever will. He suffered for me and all the redeemed. How can I be angry indefinitely with a God who loves me so much that He died for my sins? How can I stay angry when Jesus' death and resurrection ensure that my suffering will one day end? Jesus suffered for my joy today and for eternity. My battle against anger is fuelled by meditating on the unparalleled love of God. I can, by the grace of God, say 'no' to anger. And 'yes' to submission, patience, thankfulness and even joy. I must. God is helping me with this.

Before concluding, let me address an anticipated objection: 'Are you telling me that I need to simply stop feeling angry? And that I do this by simply remembering these truths?' No. And Yes.

No, I'm not telling you to stop feeling angry. I got angry when Megan died. I remember one time fleeing to my room ('fleeing' isn't too strong a word!). I had to get away from the pressures of life. I threw myself down on the bed, and proceeded to beat the mattress for maybe five minutes. All the while, I said things like: 'Why God?! Honestly!' I was angry with God. I felt aggrieved. Christians get angry with God. Of course they do. Sometimes it lasts a few minutes, sometimes longer.

So I'm not saying 'stop feeling angry!' What I am saying is this: train yourself to think and feel better. Counter your feelings of anger with truth. Slow down and live by faith. Reading the truths above won't, necessarily, change your feelings or make you happy. You have to choose. With one breath, like me, you may say: 'I hate this, God. How could you?' And, in the next breath say, 'But I trust you God. Help me. Thank you that Jesus suffered for me.'

We need to respond to our anger by believing, speaking and acting on truth. Don't the Psalms of lament do precisely this? Read Psalms 44, 60, 74, 86, and more. These poems overflow with pain, heartache, and anger. Yet they are also tremendous declarations of faith.

Sarah Edwards had reasons to be angry. Her husband, the brilliant pastor-theologian Jonathan, was taken from her by a smallpox vaccination that went wrong. Sarah's response, written to her daughter Esther, models biblical restraint and biblical faith. She could have been perpetually angry. She wasn't. Hear her words: 'What shall I say? A holy and good God has covered us with a dark cloud. O that we may kiss the rod, and lay our hands on our mouths! The Lord has done it. He has made me adore His goodness, that we had him so long. But my God lives; and He has my heart. O what a legacy my husband,

and your father, has left us! We are all given to God; and there I am, and love to be.' [16] Amen.

---

16 Iain Murray, *Jonathan Edwards: A New Biography*, The Banner of Truth Trust, 1987, pg442.

16) A group project

In school and at uni, I didn't like 'group' projects. Maybe it's research and a co-written essay? Or maybe it's a presentation in front of the rest of the class? I know there's value to this sort of thing, but I struggled to see it. I especially loathed these projects when the teacher handpicked the groups. Being with your mates at least made the experience a bit more pleasant, but partnering with strangers felt like downright torture.

What exactly didn't I like about these group projects? First of all, I didn't like that my success (or failure) was tied to others. I had to depend on them. Their hard work or their laziness affected me. It sounds selfish (maybe it is?), but if these other people fail to come through, it meant more work for me.

I also didn't like having to coordinate my schedule with theirs. I couldn't just do the work when I wanted to. If they waited to the last minute to do their bit, I was left holding the bag.

Lastly (and maybe this was the toughest pill to swallow), I have a certain independent spirit - I like to do things my way. But getting my way is just not possible when you're working with other people. I had to listen to their ideas, and do things I didn't want to do. In sum, group projects meant inconvenience for me.

Now, before you go too far 'tut tutting' my selfish take on group projects, who of us hasn't felt this way? In the office? On the pitch? In our family? Or, if we're really honest, in our church? Read back through those previous two paragraphs and exchange 'group project' for 'work team' or 'family,' and you're more than likely to sense some resonance with your own life. We all have a hard time working with others! Kinda makes you sick when you think about it.

God has made man to be a 'group project.' Your life is not, merely, a private story with you as the main actor. You were created to live alongside and work with others. I could explain, from the Bible, the truth of this statement for all humanity, but for now I have a more narrow focus in mind: God made his people *for* the local church. Your life, Christian, is a 'group' project. Better stated, your life is a church project.

During Megan's hospitalisation, this truth came home with fresh intensity and practical relevance. Of course I needed my family, especially my children, and Megan's family, too. But hear me clearly: I also needed the folks from St Giles just as much, if not more. I know I'm prone to hyperbole, but I'm really not sure if my family and I would have survived apart from the church.

Christians need the church. The New Testament assumes this interconnectedness and interdependency almost every time it speaks of the church. Let's get a sampling. I'm prone to sin, and I *need* the accountability (and sometimes chastening) of the local church (Gal. 6:1; Mt. 18:15–20). My burdens can't be borne on my own, I *need* others to help deal with the issues of life (Gal. 6:2). I *need* the church (not just the elders) to teach me God's Word (Col. 3:15–17), or my growth towards maturity as a Christian will be stunted. I *need* the comfort that comes as others weep with me and rejoice with me through life sorrows and joys (Rom. 12:15). I'm commanded not to neglect church meetings and to submit to the church's elders (Heb. 10:25; 13:17) because I *need* the routines of the preached Word, corporate worship, the sacraments and the oversight of godly men. When temptation presses in, I *need* the prayers of my brothers and sisters (Eph. 6:13). And because I am naturally selfish, I *need* to generously give my hard-earned money in support of my local church and the spread of the gospel around the world (2 Cor. 8:1–15).

I could go on. Our lives as Christians are a group project. Scripture assumes and mandates that Christians get on following Jesus *in* committed relationships with your brothers and sisters. Why would you not want to live life enmeshed in a local church?

Whilst Megan was in hospital, I wrote the following words. It might be hard, reading these words, to feel the intensity of that time, but hear the desperation I felt then for the church:

> I really need the church right now. And they have been there! I don't mean just one or two of the paid staff team. I mean everybody. One couple (with a relatively new baby themselves) is watching our dog. Many are making meals. Others have watched our children, texted, prayed, sat with me, and pointed me to Christ. Another couple (who used to be members, but moved to Northern Ireland) are bringing a pizza meal from Belfast. This is the local church: a group of

people, saved by Jesus who live in roughly the same location (that's key) and are committed to each other for each other's spiritual and practical good to the glory of God. It's like a little outpost of heaven on earth.

To use worldly terms, my family and I were experiencing something like hell, but our church gave us a taste of heaven.

I started this reflection listing all the reasons why I struggled with group projects as a student. If you look back through those reasons, I think you'll find dangerous resonance with the reasons some aren't committed to a local church. Oh, we'd never say the following things, but we've felt them: 'I don't want my life's success or failure tied to others. Working with others is inconvenient and makes more work for me. I want to do what I want, not what others want.' In the secular, independent West, this is the air we breathe. The Bible's teaching on the church militates against it, and it does so for our good.

If you're a Christian, are you a member of a local church? I hope you are. Not a viewer of an online church. Not an audience member at a satellite campus where the pastor preaching on the screen doesn't know you because he's never seen you. Not your own 'church' at home. Not a solo Christian. You need the local church to obey Jesus, be more like Jesus. You need it for moments like the one I went through.

I love the local church in all it's messiness. I love the real people who are really committed to me for my spiritual good. I'm committed to theirs, too. I love how we pray with and for each other and seek to share the gospel together. I love that they love me and my family. I love that my children love our church because our church has obviously loved them time and again. They saw it very tangibly during that tumultuous week. These people are so dear to us. I'm, in my mind, seeing people in our local church as I write this. Real people committed to each other for the sake of the gospel. That's the church.

This kind of love and commitment brings glory to God and can't help but be noticed by the outside world. The nurses around Megan saw this. So did our neighbours and friends both local and abroad. They couldn't believe our church. Paul, in Ephesians 3:20-21, declares that God is deserving of glory. Hear where this glory is made manifest: 'Now to him who is able to do far more abundantly than all that we ask or think, according to the power at work within us, to him be glory in the church and in Christ Jesus throughout all generations, forever and ever.' To God be glory in the church.

In that fateful week, I was struck by this theme. I so desperately wanted God to be glorified in healing Megan. That didn't happen, but he was glorified in ways I didn't anticipate. Here's what I wrote at the time:

> Guys, God may still miraculously heal my wife. Pray that he does. But have his miraculous power and glory not already been displayed – in the church and in Christ over these last few days through so many of you? You, my fellow saints, have been born again by a work of the Holy Spirit – a miracle! You have trusted in a glorious Saviour who died for your sins – a miracle! You have lived together as a believing community and inconvenienced yourselves for each other – yep, miracle again! Starting to see the picture? Megan would want me to

talk about her healing, but even more she would want me to talk about the miracles we see every day (and forget) to the glory of God. God has, is, and will be glorified in his church and in Christ Jesus for all generations, forever and ever! Even here in our hospital ward.

Let me close like this. Do you love the local church like Jesus? Do you love her enough to inconvenience yourself for her and commit to her? It pays off. You may not like group projects, but you need them. At least one, you do.

Section 2: The Days That Followed

The unthinkable had indeed happened. Megan really was gone. Once she actually died, a whole new period of grief was ushered in. We missed her *and* we had to carry on without her. The days in hospital were intense, but this was something altogether different. The section that follows reflects on this intense period, the 'days that followed.'

The early days after Megan's death are largely a blur. But one memory persists: everyday, we checked in on our newborn. The hospital kindly kept him in the neonatal intensive care unit till after his mum's funeral. In God's kindness, he wasn't there for the sake of his health. They allowed him to stay there for my sake, and to allow us to make preparations to bring him home. All told, he was there just over two weeks. Through that time, the presence of family was a constant source of help and encouragement.

Ten days after Megan died, we held a thanksgiving service, and we were overwhelmed by how many joined us. Friends, family, fellow church members, a number of caring acquaintances – so many came! Let me give a few examples. A good friend from America traveled across the Atlantic to join us, leaving behind his family and his work for a couple of days. A number of our unbelieving neighbours joined us. Three teachers from our son's secondary school came. The imam from the local prison where for a few years I'd led Bible studies even came along.

But most of all, we were pleased to see two nurses from the critical care ward. What a sad but joyful day – that sounds weird, but it's true. As I hinted at earlier, we wanted to fervently sing songs filled with biblical truth. Praise God, we did. And our friend, Mike, preached the gospel clearly and powerfully. We were directed to the hope that can only be had in the crucified and resurrected Saviour, and the lost were called upon to turn from sin to Christ in faith. It was exhausting and refreshing.

The graveside service followed three days later. Megan was buried in a church yard in rural Kent. I had the privilege of serving as the assistant pastor there for a brief period, and the same church, long dear to our hearts, graciously allowed us to bury Megan in their graveyard. For a January day, the weather was surprisingly clear, even if it was cold. We prayed, we sang and we were again reminded of our hope in the Lord Jesus, the one who conquered death and the grave.

We returned home, and began the process of getting back to some sort of 'normal life.' Our grief was immense, and life with seven children was full. For three months, Megan's mum joined us. I can't imagine what we would have done without her help. We saw God's provision in so many obvious ways, but our grief persisted.

Section 2: The Days That Followed

These chapters aim to help us grieve well in and through the early, trying days of loss. When the unthinkable has happened, we're often left reeling. It's during this intense period that we need help to grieve *well*.

when sorrows like sea billows roll

17) It's all about who you know

Was there anything particularly special about my response to Megan's death? I'm not sure. Maybe? I'm pretty sure I experienced the same sort of emotions as anybody, and I know for sure that some of the difficult practicalities we faced are not unique. Still, it seemed like many were surprised by how I carried myself in the days after Megan died. I know that I'm quirky (my family and friends can a bit too happily confirm this!), but people were noticing something more than just my peculiar personality. How do I know that people were surprised? Because they told me.

I had had this sort of conversation at least a dozen times during those days, but I remember one particular instance quite vividly. It was a few months after Megan's death, and there was a dramatic performance on at the primary school. Chris and I were walking across a churchyard en route to a cheeky, pre-performance coffee. We had 20 minutes to burn, just enough time for Chris to ask his burning question. To put this in perspective: Chris is a Christian. We'd had friendly, casual interactions before this, and he'd followed the circumstances surrounding Megan's death. His question went something like this: 'I just don't get it. How can you respond to Megan's death like this?' As Chris coloured in his question, it became clear what he was asking.

Let me paraphrase the ensuing conversation for you, cutting through the typical British reserve: 'Your beloved wife just traumatically died. You have seven children (including a newborn!). How are you not utterly broken? Why are you not a gooey mess on the floor right about now? Because I think I would be.' Pardon my colourful language, but I don't think that's too far off from what Chris and others communicated at that time. Onlookers were intrigued by how I, my family and our church responded to this situation.

Pause there for a sec. How do I write this and not sound self-congratulatory? How can I write this and it not come off as saying: 'Weren't we great?' Quite frankly, this feels like a danger in *all* that I've written here. I am, after all, writing a book about my experiences, my responses and the lessons to be learnt from all of it.

But hear me clearly: I'm praying that this book and these reflections drive you to say: 'Wow, isn't God great!' not 'Wow, isn't Brad great!' I'm praying that my example drives you back to God and his word in your imminent times of suffering. Follow my example, in so far as I follow Christ (1 Cor. 11:1). This reflection could sound like boasting. I get that. But I'm happy to have a go and walk the knife's edge between boasting and using my life as an illustration, praying that it's fruitful for you. Let the reader understand.

Back to Chris' question. He wanted to know how I was so calm, happy, and high-functioning. Conversely, why was I not more depressed, more frazzled and just plain debilitated? To put me in my place for a sec, Chris didn't see me *all of the time*. He didn't see the very late night (mornings?) when my newborn was painfully awake. I was not so happy and more than a little frazzled then!

But I think Chris was generally right. I was as he described me. People noticed. I knew they noticed, and I knew the reason to the question. Let me just state it clearly: there's a direct relationship between how well you know God and how well you handle grief. To put it differently: Your stability amidst times of suffering depends on your personal acquaintance with the living God.

Knowing God does not double as a 'get out of suffering free' card, nor does it evacuate suffering of its sorrow. Nonetheless, if you know God well, then your response to suffering will be transformed. Yes, the ship of your life will still be blown about by the storms, but you'll have a steadier hand at the helm. I know God, and what I know of him provided a stability to my life during those tumultuous days.

Do you? How do you *know* if you know God? I could quiz you on your Bible knowledge. I could tabulate your church attendance or investigate the physical state of your Bible. All of these may give hints as to whether you know the Lord, but they'd be inconclusive.

But God has given us a simple indicator to help us determine how well we know him: our suffering. Your suffering exposes your practical theology like few other means. Think back to the last hard thing you faced. How did you respond? What did

101

you say? How did you feel? If you're not sure, ask your church family to help you remember and evaluate. Did you sound like Habakkuk as he anticipated Judah's sacking at the hands of Babylon?

> Though the fig-tree does not bud and there are no grapes on the vines, though the olive crop fails and the fields produce no food, though there are no sheep in the sheepfold and no cattle in the stalls, yet I will rejoice in the Lord, I will be joyful in God my Saviour (Hab. 3:17-18).

Did your thoughts, words and actions reflect the Psalmist in Psalm 73? 'Whom have I in heaven but you? And earth has nothing I desire besides you. My flesh and my heart may fail, but God is the strength of my heart and my portion for ever' (vv25–26). These two writers knew the Lord. They saw God as supremely valuable, almighty, good, and holy. Thus their pain took on a different hue. The bigger your view is of God, the smaller you see your suffering. The more you view life with correct proportion, the more steady and stable you are under fire.

This is the answer I tried to give to Chris and others during those days. What about you? Where can you start to get such a big view of God?

A few recommendations. First, read the book of Job slowly. You will meet with a God who is sovereign and holy. Job should lead its readers to stunned silence before God (Job 42:1–6). Second, read Isaiah 40–48. Ask yourself the question: who really is like God? To whom will you compare him (Is. 40:25-26, etc)?

If you'd like to read a couple books that will raise your estimation of God and equip you to know him better, here are three accessible resources: *Knowing God* by JI Packer, *The Holiness of God* by RC Sproul and *The Pleasures of God* by John Piper. These three books have helped me immensely.

Now for the practical exhortation. Let me urge you to pray and ask God to make himself known to you. Plead with God to help you by His Spirit to know Him better. I don't know, fundamentally, that my response to Megan's death was that different from other Christians in similar positions. But by the grace of God, I *do* know the Lord. And there's no doubt this profoundly affected my response to my situation. Let me urge you: get to know God better. See him in all his glory. Don't settle for an insufficient view of God. The smaller your view of God, the bigger and badder your hardships will appear.

when sorrows like sea billows roll

18) Companionship

I didn't have sufficient words to describe how I tangibly felt Megan's absence. I still don't think I do. At the time, I described it as a 'continual, dull ache in my chest.' That's close, but inexact, insufficient.

I couldn't figure out how to explain how much I sensed her *physical* absence, that I missed her so much that it *physically* hurt. I suppose you could simply say that I missed Megan. I just wanted her there, and she wasn't.

Strangely, the ache has muted over time, but it hasn't gone away. I still want Megan here, and she isn't. Every now and then, especially powerful moments come over me unexpectedly, and I freshly ache for Megan. On those days, I almost say to myself: 'Did she *really* die?' Only to realise all over again, 'Oh yeah, of course she did.' Sometimes, it's almost like I expect her to come in the lounge from the kitchen carrying a biscuit and a cuppa, and I'm surprised when I remember that she won't – and she never will again.

For 14 years, Megan and I were almost inseparable. Every joy and every sorrow, we shared together. When something good happened, she found out first; when hard times came, she was always there to commiserate. We were by each other's side through five house moves (including one across the Atlantic), various academic courses, seven pregnancies and child-births, the ups and downs of Christian ministry, holidays, illnesses, injuries, and all of life's big decisions and mundane trivialities. She was always there. Next to me in bed each night or a phone call away.

Some of our times together were particularly lovely; our tenth anniversary trip to Greece stands out. Our feet hurt from all the walking we did together, but our hearts were full of thanks to God for giving us each other. We were together. Our marriage was full of all sorts of sweet moments like that.

We also had our fair share of bitter providences. Before the tumultuous period around New Year, we thought we'd reached the high watermark of the 'floods' of suffering. For three years early in our marriage, we bore up together under what seemed at the time to be severe ministry pressures. We were pushed to the edge, and yet the Lord sustained us. Then, a few years later, Megan had an ectopic pregnancy. That was hard. Then, a year later, we very nearly had to leave our home and our church as Her Majesty's Government felt very strongly that our visas should no longer be valid (long story). Kindly, the Home Office gave us 60 days to sort another visa and, just in time, we did. Phew. 'Let's not do that sort of thing again!' we naively said to each other. I could go on, but you get the point – Megan and I suffered *together*. Our shared experiences both good and bad deepened and sweetened our love.

Through it all, we'd been together – and now we weren't. My best friend was gone.

In those early days after her death, practically everything about my daily routine reminded me of this. Let me give two examples: at bedtime, we'd had a routine whereby Megan and I would kiss each other goodnight, but then one or both of us would make air kisses before we'd actually turn out the lights. I'm kinda mortified to write this, but it does illustrate what I'm driving at! This bedtime routine was something we shared, just the two of us. After Megan died, I think I continued kissing the air every night at lights out for six months.

My second example centres on parenting. I missed Megan most when it came to parenting. Besides the comedic fact that I had to raise a newborn practically *on my own* (picture that for a second!), parenting our children brought me to tears more than anything in those early days. You can probably picture me holding a newborn, calling for a 3-year-old whilst pulling my 13- and 9-year-olds off each other.

Of course, every parent keenly feels their shortcomings. I experienced the added complication that every time I felt inadequate, I also remembered that my partner in parenting was no longer at my side. Boy, did I need her. I can't tell you how many times I cried (and then cried out to God) during and after difficult parenting moments! I haven't even mentioned that just *seeing* the children reminded me she was no longer there; they looked so much like her. She was a brilliant companion through all of life, and so her memory hovered over every aspect of life.

This all makes sense. Companionship is one of the purposes for which God, in his wisdom, ordained marriage. *The Book of Common Prayer* beautifully summarises God's purposes for marriage. I quote from it (in a slightly amended form) whenever I have the privilege of officiating at a wedding. Here's what I say at almost every wedding. It's familiar language:

> Dear family and friends, we're gathered together here in the sight of God, and in the face of this congregation to join together this man and this woman in holy matrimony; which is an honourable estate, instituted by God in the time of man's innocency. Marriage was designed to signify to us the spiritual union between Christ and his Church, and Scripture commends it to be honoured by all people. Marriage is not to be participated in lightly, hastily, or wantonly – to satisfy men's carnal lusts and appetites; but reverently, discreetly, advisedly, soberly and in the fear of God; rightly considering the cause for which marriage was ordained: First, marriage was ordained for the procreation of children, to be brought up in the discipline and instruction of the Lord and to the praise of His holy name. Secondly, it was ordained for a remedy against sin, and to avoid fornication; that those who struggle with self-control might marry, and keep themselves pure and undefiled members of Christ's body. Thirdly, it was ordained for the good of both the husband and the wife, for their mutual joy; for the help and comfort given one another in times of adversity and prosperity. It is into this holy union that _____ and _____ now come to be joined.[17]

---

17 *The Book of Common Prayer: the Texts of 1549, 1559, and 1662* edited by Brian Cummings, Oxford University Press, 2013, pg 157. The language and spellings have been slightly modernised.

I really couldn't say it better myself (which is why I don't try!). Read again, slowly, the third 'cause' for which marriage was ordained. It's a beautiful way of saying that marriage was ordained for 'companionship.' Marriage was created by God, in part, so that men and women wouldn't have to fly solo. So that you and I would have a companion through life. So that you wouldn't be alone while experiencing the joys and sorrows of life. Remember what God declared when he created Adam? 'The Lord God said, 'It is not good for the man to be alone. I will make a helper suitable for him' (Gen. 2:18). It isn't good to be alone. God's answer to this problem? Marriage. What a wonderful invention. How wise and good God is.

This truth is simple enough, but I think it's under-appreciated today. Maybe it's our modern, Western fixation on sex and our high view of individual autonomy? I'm not sure. I *do* know that after Megan died, I came to appreciate this third purpose for marriage like never before. I didn't realise how good I had it. Gone were the help and comfort Megan gave to me. Here I was facing an unparalleled adversity, and my usual source of joy, help and comfort was gone. My companion, God's gracious gift to me, was gone.

Let me offer a few points of application. First, married couples: don't underestimate the tremendous gift you have in your husband or wife! You, through thick and thin, have a companion. Amidst the tensions of married life and the ever-present reality of sin in our everyday interactions, it's so easy to forget just what God has given to you. Marriage is hard, but let's not lose sight of the fact that marriage is good. So work to cultivate a thankful heart today. We're told to 'Rejoice always ... give thanks in all circumstances; for this is God's will for you in Christ Jesus' (1 Thes. 5:16,18). It's time to put this into practice regarding your spouse. Maybe you need to write out a list of all the things you're thankful for about your him or her? In a moment, your companion could be taken away.

Second, take practical, everyday steps to foster your friendship with your spouse. Megan and I were closer 14 years into marriage than we were on our wedding day. But don't forget that companionship must also be cultivated. The Teacher tells us: 'Though one may be overpowered, two can defend themselves. A cord of three strands is not quickly broken' (Ecc. 4:12). This proverb is self-explanatory, but the question for us is simple: are we labouring to daily weave the 'cord' of our life together with our husband or wife? Everyday you make choices that will either breed companionship or stunt it. Carve out time together, cut off habits or hobbies that come between you, and be strategic in loving and serving your spouse in ways that will encourage your relationship. The hard work will pay off.

Lastly, if you are unmarried and you long for a spouse/a companion, pray for one, and where appropriate seek after one with the input of your church family. You are no less a person if you are not married, but if you desire to be married, you should take steps towards getting married. I know, I know. You don't *have* to get married. That's true. We tell young Christians this all the time. Unmarried Christians aren't second-class Christians. But I wonder if we've failed to also tell our young people, 'Hey, it's really good to be married!' Because it is!

19) With the comfort we ourselves receive

'I'm sorry, I'm going to have to get my colleague to take over for me. I just can't do this.'

That's what the attendant at the Job Centre Plus told me. She spoke through teary eyes. This reaction came after she'd asked for clarification: 'I don't think I understand. Can you please explain your family situation to me?' The moment I heard this question, I knew where this conversation would end, but I didn't expect *this*. I'd become used to this kind of reaction in the months that followed Megan's death.

Let me give some background.

I was at the Job Centre Plus because our family circumstances had obviously changed. Any benefits and tax credits we were receiving would have to be re-evaluated. This required an in-person appointment. Now, the Job Centre Plus is rarely a happy place. But I came prepared. I had all the appropriate paperwork filled in, and all the necessary supporting documents.

The aforementioned attendant looked over my application, but she still couldn't figure out why I was there. Hence her clarification question, and my explanation of Megan's untimely death. As I recounted our story, I could see her getting more choked up.

The attendant, at first, asked an unprofessional but appropriate question that I was getting a lot then: 'How are you able to cope? Do you have help?' I responded as best I could on the fly and was able to bear something of a testimony to God's goodness through the help of our church family. I frankly don't remember what I said. I too was a little emotional by that time! At some point along the way, this woman completely broke down, unable to go on. She hastily pulled her colleague into conversation, and I shifted over to the adjacent cubicle. And then, somewhat surreally, I had to explain to this second attendant why his colleague had reacted and so I again explained our family's story. He was visibly moved but able to carry on.

The first attendant literally couldn't. She gave it her best shot, but she just couldn't. Maybe she'd already had a hard day? It's hard for me to even *visit* the Job Centre Plus, it's surely harder to *work* there! Maybe our story had some specific resonance with her own? Maybe she was just overcome by Megan's surprising death and the thought of a single dad with seven children? I don't know. I do know her reaction was not atypical.

Those close to us were, understandably, mourning Megan's death, but so too were strangers. Fellow parents at the school, friends of friends, and even the bank associate (I had to go and change our account information). So many were shocked, dismayed and grieved by Megan's death. Some would try to speak with me, only to find themselves at a loss for words. Others would simply start crying in my presence. Maybe it was just me, but the frequency seemed telling.

How do you respond in this situation? You are grieving, and people know that. But they're grieving, too – both with you and for you. One response is to do nothing. Grieve and let grieve. That's not necessarily bad. Another response? Avoid people, or at least avoid the painful topic as much as possible. That was often my response. I avoided the topic of Megan's death. I didn't want to have to explain. I didn't want to have to deal with other people's emotional reactions. Sometimes, I'd ask a conversation partner: 'Have you heard our story?' and I'd be relieved when they had! It meant I didn't have to freshly stir up all those emotions (in me and in them!). This second reaction also isn't necessarily bad, but it's not a good solution long-term.

So what *do* you do? How can you react to others who feel bad about and are saddened by your grief?

Before we get some help in this area, let me put out there one thing I wish I'd thought of earlier: I wish I'd recognised that I didn't have to pastor *everybody* through their sorrow. I struggled with this. I tried at first, and found it exhausting. Free yourself with this thought: you obviously can't, nor should you try to pastor everyone. Of course, you have natural responsibility for your family, your church, etc. But every person's grief is not necessarily your responsibility.

So how *do* you react? How do you respond to the Job Centre Plus employee, the parent that breaks down at the school gate or even to your fellow church member who doesn't really know what to say? I want to recommend one key thought and one practical step.

The key thought: your suffering (especially your bereavement) is rarely your suffering alone. Others will often be changed by what you go through. Your family, friends, church family and others will grieve for you and alongside you. They will feel bad, and they will feel bad that you feel bad. They will ache and grieve. This is hard to remember when your world seems to be crumbling in on you , when you miss your departed wife, mother or child.

Let me state it differently (and push it slightly further): your loss is not an excuse for selfishness. We love to talk about how our suffering is unique, and we therefore deserve to get our way. This idea must be shunned; our suffering doesn't lead to entitlement. Paul tells us: 'And we urge you, brothers and sisters, warn those who are idle and disruptive, encourage the disheartened, help the weak, be patient with everyone' (1 Thes. 5:14). Does this responsibility change when we've encountered the death of a loved one? Our suffering, Christians, must not turn us inward. We can encourage the disheartened, help the weak and be patient with everyone. We must.

This leads into the practical step: comfort those around you in whatever way you can. Or, to riff on John Piper's phrase: 'Don't waste your bereavement.' The apostle Paul, again, urges us this way: 'Praise be to the God and Father of our Lord Jesus Christ, the Father of compassion and the God of all comfort, who comforts us in all our troubles, so that we can comfort those in any trouble with the comfort we ourselves receive from God' (2 Cor. 1:3-4). Do you see Paul's logic? Our Heavenly Father comforts us. Surely you've known the comfort of God in previous trials. Why does He comfort us? So that we can pass that comfort on. Don't waste your bereavement. In your suffering, as hard as it is, turn outward. Use this season to serve others.

What does this look like? Lots of things. Here is a shortlist:

1. Share bits of Scripture that have sustained you. If Matthew 12:20 ('A bruised reed he will not break, and a smouldering wick he will not snuff out') encouraged your heart, share that with someone else. I mean, isn't it lovely that Jesus is gentle with bruised reeds and smouldering wicks like us?

2. Simply listen to others. Don't be caught off-guard or surprised that they're struggling, too. Pay attention to their reflections on their pain and your pain – it's very likely you'll learn from them. To put it more bluntly: try not to be put off by other people struggling to deal with a hard situation.

3. Pray for those grieving. What better way to turn outward than to ask the Lord to help and bless others who are struggling? Do you see how this takes the attention off you and puts it on God and others?

4. Bear testimony to God's goodness in the midst of hard times. What obvious good has God done for you? Did somebody slip you a fiver, and it was just enough for your dinner? Did your dad buy you a new suit for the funeral (mine did, and I'm really thankful!)? Did you have

a moment of ecstasy as you remembered the wonderful times you spent with your now-deceased friend? Speak about these things with others.

5. See your suffering as an opportunity to point others to Jesus Christ. What more comforting truth is there than the fact that our sin was dealt with comprehensively and graciously on the cross? We are bound for eternity before the face of God, escaping the judgement of God, purely on the basis of the mercy of God. Speak about this to Christians and non-Christians alike. Turn outward. In other words, take the comfort you've received and comfort others with it.

Jesus famously says, 'Blessed are those who mourn, for they will be comforted' (Mt. 5:4). Clearly, Jesus is pointing forward to the heavenly comfort to be enjoyed one day by Christians who mourn now. I wonder too, though, if part of the comfort Jesus promises comes today. I reckon it does, and it comes at least in part by you sharing the comfort you've already received. Do you get that? As you share something of the comfort you've received, you yourself are comforted now. It's an upward spiral of comfort. Take Jesus at his word – yes, even at the Job Centre Plus.

20) More valuable than ravens

God will meet the needs of His people. Always and without fail.

Every Christian affirms this. 'Of course He will,' we say. But the problem comes when hard times strike. When the unthinkable happens, we wonder: 'This time, will I really have what I need?'

Consider these 'unthinkable' situations, which are reality for more people than we realise: Armed conflict breaks out in your country, and national food supplies dwindle. Will your children have enough to eat? Your company restructures and you've suddenly been made redundant. The job prospects in your field are small, and you feel like you're too old to retrain. Will you be able to keep your flat? Your mum dies, and her tender care and quiet encouragement are gone. Will you be able to get on without her?

What happens when we just can't see how this situation could actually work out. Oh, we *believe* God will provide, but we have no idea how that could possibly happen. We wonder if he won't, and even if he does, we wonder if it'll still be painful.

Let's rehearse the Bible's teaching on this point. Can we be sure of God's provision in *all* circumstances? In short: yes. God's people will always have what they need when they need it. Painful circumstances don't derail God's provision. This certainty is rooted in God's nature as universal creator and sustainer: 'All creatures look to you to give them their food at the proper time. When you give it to them, they gather it up; when you open your hand, they are satisfied with good things' (Ps. 104:27–28). If you ate lunch today, God provided it. If the wild goat in the Andes mountains found grass this morning, God provided it. Of course, the young man at the sandwich shop prepared the coronation chicken sarnie you paid for, but God provided that sandwich just as much as He provided grass for that Andean goat! All creatures (even those who don't realise it) look to God to give them food at the proper time.

Jesus applied this truth even more directly. He says, 'Consider the ravens: They do not sow or reap, they have no storeroom or barn; yet God feeds them. And how much more valuable you are than birds!' (Lk. 12:24) Jesus' point is clear: if God feeds the ravens, then he will definitely feed His redeemed children. The ravens matter to God, but His people matter more.

God will meet your needs, Christian. Always. 'He who did not spare his own Son, but gave him up for us all – how will he not also, along with him, graciously give us all things?' (Rom. 8:32) He gave us the most costly gift, his Son. Everything else is gravy. You can depend on Him.

In the days after Megan's death, I saw this truth with fresh clarity. Though I too struggled to believe it, God kept His promise and provided for our family. Our needs were met and then some. Praise God. So I'm writing this chapter not merely to report this truth, but to testify that I have seen it with my eyes (Job 42:5).

So how exactly did God provide for us?

First, the body of Christ met our needs. Real people give very practical services and tangible goods. Scripture puts this expectation on believers. James says that true religion is to take care of brothers and sisters (especially widows and orphans) in need (Jas. 1:27). Jesus magnifies the significance of this by saying that to care for brothers and sisters amongst us is as if you've cared for Jesus himself (Mt. 25:38). In fact, this kind of love distinguishes His disciples from the rest of the world (Jn. 13:35).

Summary: meeting each other's practical needs should be normal amongst Christians, and we can actually go so far as to expect God to use our brothers and sisters when we have needs. This is exactly our story. God used our church family and other Christians to provide for our needs in abundance. Here's a short list of what we were given: childcare, three months' worth of meals (for a family of eight, that's a lot of food!), encouraging notes, lifts, runs to the shops, some stayed the night, others let us stay over at theirs and so many prayed for us. God moves His people to meet each other's needs. Count on it.

Second, God commonly meets His people's needs by his people just working hard. God told Adam: 'By the sweat of our brow, you will eat your food' (Gen. 3:19). The principle shows up repeatedly in Proverbs: 'A sluggard's appetite is never filled, but the desires of the diligent are fully satisfied' (13:4). We need to remember this principle both in trials and the trivialities of our normal life. We reap what we sow. As we work hard, God uses our efforts to provide for our own family's needs.

We worked really hard during that season, and God met our needs. Both are true. How many books do you know that tell you to work hard during times of trial? Probably not many, but isn't this realistic? You doubt whether God will provide for your needs. You can't see where the help you need will come from. God will provide for you as you work hard. It's not easy, but count on it.

Finally, God provides for us by giving us unexpected gifts. God provides for the cattle and the young ravens (Ps. 147:9), and so he provided for us. Sometimes, he provides for us in unforeseen ways. I cannot relay to you (let alone remember!) how much this happened in those days after Megan's death. Let me give a few examples.

While Megan was in critical care, we'd eat out near the hospital. We needed sustenance, but we wanted to be close by in case of emergency. Well, eating out costs money (a lot of money, actually!). Very kindly, a friend slipped me an envelope with a couple of hundred quid in it and told me to use it for whatever needs might arise. As you might now guess, I used that money for these meals out. Remarkably, that money ran out the day Megan died. It still makes me shiver to think that every meal we needed was covered. And it got even crazier than that. Over the course of a few days, £50,000 was donated to our family via a crowdfunding site. I mean, who saw that coming? Not me.

God had provided for us in abundance – in ways I never could have foreseen! Over the months that followed, that 50k paid for family travel expenses, baby supplies, childcare, etc. What a gift! Our needs were met and then some.

One more unexpected, but more mundane gift came by way of school. Before Megan's death, we'd homeschooled our children. Obviously that was no longer an option, and Megan's death left me scrambling. What are the odds I'd find places for three children in the same school in precisely the years I needed? I'll spell it out for you: the odds are low. Yet God provided. You can't always foresee just how God will provide for you, but He will. Count on it.

Let me close this reflection with two bits of advice. When you look out over the vista of your life, and you can't imagine how things could possibly work out, remember the ravens. When you don't know how your needs will be met, remember the ravens. You are more valuable to God than they are. Lean on your church family, work hard and expect the unexpected. God will provide. You really can count on it. Even if He doesn't provide in the ways you *think you need*, you can be sure he will give you what you *actually* need.

Second, humble yourself before the Lord, and trust Him amidst your anxiety. 'Humble yourselves, therefore, under God's mighty hand, that he may lift you up in due time. Cast all your anxiety on him because he cares for you' (1 Pet. 5:6–7). I admit it: I don't have this down. But it's what I aim for. It takes humility to trust the Lord in uncertain days. As you think less of yourself and your needs by thinking more about God and His past faithfulness to His promises, He will exalt you.

Read that last sentence again. Truth be told: you may be at a low point right now, but you will be lifted up. God really does care for you. His hand is mighty. God will meet the needs of His people. Always and without fail.

21) You will be my witnesses

Just before ascending into heaven, Jesus said to his disciples: "'But you will receive power when the Holy Spirit comes on you; and you will be my witnesses in Jerusalem, and in all Judea and Samaria, and to the ends of the earth'" (Acts 1:8). They would bear witness for Jesus to people all over the world. As the church in the book of Acts understood, this commission extends beyond the twelve. All disciples of Jesus in all ages and places have the privilege of being Jesus' witnesses. That means you and me.

As the early days of the New Testament church unfolded, it became clear that this witnessing would not take place in the context of comfort, ease and adulation. What Jesus said earlier proved true: the gospel will spread in the midst of suffering and persecution.

> You must be on your guard. You will be handed over to the local councils and flogged in the synagogues. On account of me you will stand before governors and kings as witnesses to them. And the gospel must first be preached to all nations. Whenever you are arrested and brought to trial, do not worry beforehand about what to say. Just say whatever is given you at the time, for it is not you speaking, but the Holy Spirit.

Brother will betray brother to death, and a father his child. Children will rebel against their parents and have them put to death. Everyone will hate you because of me, but the one who stands firm to the end will be saved (Mk. 13:9–13).

The normal context for the spread of the gospel is suffering, trials and even death. What does this mean for us today?

Of course, many of our brothers and sisters around the world would hear this and be tempted to respond, 'Well, duh, of course it does.' Evangelism always goes with suffering, or at least the threat of it. To speak of Jesus or to 'proselytise' is a punishable offence in much of the world. While we may seem to be heading that way in the West, we are certainly not there yet. The relative freedom and safety we've enjoyed has caused us to forget the pattern of the New Testament. Suffering and evangelism go together. In fact, suffering is a ripe opportunity to evangelise.

I don't remember reading a book on evangelism that makes this connection. I know of books that urge you to be bold amidst an anti-gospel, cultural tidal wave. But I don't know of evangelism books that urge you to utilise your suffering for evangelistic purposes. I also don't know of books on suffering that make this connection.

So perhaps this perspective is needed: Christian, you should leverage your suffering for evangelism. Bear testimony for Jesus in life's challenging moments. Of course, you'll be hurting. But even amidst the hurt, you should tell others about Jesus. I feel strangely harsh saying as much. But then I think of the Apostle

Paul and the other disciples in Acts. Did these saints endure tremendous suffering? Let's consider the biblical record.

In Acts 12, we read the first of the Twelve to be put to death. James meets his end at the hands of the immoral and conniving King Herod (v2). What a sad day this must have been for the Twelve, let alone for John. After all, James was his brother! Of course there had been other martyrs before (think Stephen), but this is the first of the Twelve. Those men that spent three years in the company of the Lord. To make matters worse, James' murder is followed by Peter's imprisonment (vv3–5). Despite Peter's eventual, miraculous release, this episode must have been hard for the fledgling church.

Amidst all of this, you might expect the Christians to press the pause button on their work of witnessing. Nope. We read in Acts 12:24: 'But the word of God continued to spread and flourish.' In other words, people continued to talk about Jesus and other people believed. Remarkable.

This is the normal course of action throughout the New Testament. Paul and Silas' imprisonment in Philippi leads to the conversion of the jailer and his family (Acts 16:34). Paul's letters paint a similar picture. The suffering he goes through on his missionary journeys is enough to scare off even the most stout of heart (2 Cor. 11:16–33). Yet amidst all of this, he bears witness to Jesus' death, burial and resurrection for the salvation of sinners.

The world suffers, and Christians suffer. The world watches how we respond to suffering. You don't think Peter's counsel applies only to Christians in apologetics debates, do you? 'But in your hearts revere Christ as Lord. Always be prepared to give an answer to everyone who asks you to give the reason for the hope that you have. But do this with gentleness and respect' (1 Pet. 3:15).

So, if this is the norm and the expectation, what do we do? In critical care wards, in graveyards, in tear-filled living rooms and in sombre conversations at the school gate, how can we talk about Jesus? Here are four tips I learned from the days following Megan's death. I'm not a perfect or even necessarily a good evangelist, but hopefully they will help you creatively evangelise during suffering.

Tip 1: Talk about your suffering and the people who are suffering with you.

This may be hard for some of us, but opening up about our physical and emotional challenges may prompt deeper conversation. As you talk about your wife's condition or death, it will lead people to ask how you're coping. And you can tell them. But this kind of testimony is not all I mean. I also mean: tell unbelievers about how your church is suffering with you and helping you in the struggle. In our situation, this wasn't too hard. After all, so many in our church family *visibly* suffered with us. I remember nurses and the families of other patients asking us who all these people were. And I could tell them.

Tip 2: Invite unbelievers into your suffering.

As I mentioned, I invited the critical care doctors and nurses to Megan's thanksgiving service. Praise God, two of the nurses came! I accepted help from our unbelieving neighbours.

126

Our lovely Italian neighbour made us a very nice lasagne, if I remember right. These two things, honestly, didn't require that much effort, but it brought these individuals in closer proximity to other Christians and, in the case of the funeral, gave these nurses the chance to hear the gospel.

Tip 3: Explain specifically what you believe.

This sounds simplistic, but it's not. We get scared and wimp out all the time, don't we? When someone asks you how you're coping, tell them. Tell them about your hope in the Lord Jesus. Tell that he is like an anchor for the soul that persists beyond suffering (Heb. 6:19).

Your suffering will prompt these kind of questions. When someone is awed by the care you're receiving from the church, tell them why the church does these things. Tell them about how the love you've received compels the church to love each other (2 Cor. 5:13–14). Just tell people what you believe.

Tip 4: Trust the Lord with your meagre efforts.

This may sound very basic, but it's an important reminder. We plant seed and water that seed, but God brings the growth (1 Cor. 3:6–7). We are called to be witnesses. That means we give a truthful and faithful account of what Jesus has done. The Holy Spirit takes that testimony and blesses it. Don't forget that successful evangelism doesn't mean conversions. Successful evangelism is the proclamation of the good news. Your 'meagre' efforts are pleasing to God. We are simply called to be witnesses (Acts 1:8; Mt. 28:19–20).

Think about it: you have the privilege in your suffering to speak of Jesus. In fact, your suffering may provide opportunities that you'll never have again. So seize the moment. Be bold. Tell a drowning world who the lifeguard is. Despite the pain of your hardship, speak of your Saviour who will one day tell you, 'Well done good and faithful servant' (Mt. 25:23).

22) Today's going to be a hard day

I'm not much of a crier. This probably surprised some in the days around Megan's death. I cried very rarely, and almost never in public.

But I did sometimes cry. One night in particular stands out. This time, no one saw me except my screaming 4-month-old who wouldn't get back to sleep even though it was 3 AM. As I reflect back over the whole of my life, I've had few 'dark nights of the soul,' but that night was one. In all sincerity, I felt hopeless.

Let me put that night in context. Our baby didn't handle colds well. He'd get a cold, and he'd struggle to breathe. It was hard to watch. Worse than that (if I can say that?), when he did have a cold, he couldn't keep any milk down. I'd be feeding him his bottle, a coughing fit would begin, and up would come all the milk he'd just drunk. All. Of. It. The half-digested milk would go all over me and all over the sofa or bed. It made a mess, and it didn't smell nice. Doesn't that sound fun?

I'm sure other parents have similar stories. Some poor souls, as they read this, are right now nodding in unpleasant agreement. On the night in question, the baby had just such a cold. By 3 AM, he hadn't slept for anything longer than 10 minutes. He'd fall asleep eating, and he'd wake up coughing.

This coughing would bring forth the aforementioned vomiting. Again. We'd already gone through 2-3 sheets on his cot, and just as many on my bed. Now picture me cuddling this baby and just trying to get him to sleep. I was knackered, it was the middle of the night, and all I could think about was the busy day that loomed on the morning horizon. Let's just say I didn't think there'd be time for a refreshing midday nap. In a few short hours, the other six children would wake up, and we'd be off to the races.

So I cried. It was a loud and beleaguered cry. It might be best to describe it as 'sobbing.'

I was tired, emotionally drained, and I saw no way out. I knew he would *eventually* get to sleep, but it sure didn't feel like it! Then suddenly, almost out of nowhere, two thoughts came to me. I remember them with absolute clarity, which is strange given that I was just so tired.

The first thought: 'I miss Megan.' Megan's death felt especially visceral and painful to me that night. It's sad, isn't it? One of the times I missed her most was when I felt most inconvenienced by her absence. Maybe that's common? I don't know; I just missed her. I wanted her there with me. I needed her help.

The second thought came with equal force: 'Tomorrow is going to be hard … but God will be glorified.' It's not earth-shaking, I realise. But it hit me: however hard my day was going to be, God would be glorified in it. I don't usually have thoughts like this, so praise God! This thought was a game-changer. Even in the middle of the night, it became oddly refocusing.

When suffering comes, we should expect hard days. Obviously. But think about that for a moment. Some days will just be hard.

There are lots of reasons a day can go pear-shaped. The obvious ground for this expectation is the fall of man. After Adam sinned, God promised him: 'Because you listened to your wife and ate fruit from the tree about which I commanded you, 'You must not eat from it,' Cursed is the ground because of you; through painful toil you will eat food from it all the days of your life. It will produce thorns and thistles for you, and you will eat the plants of the field' (Gen. 3:17–18). Painful toil, thorns, thistles and plant-based dinners – all hints in the direction of a few bad days. The New Testament is no less explicit. None other than Jesus promised: 'In this world you will have trouble' (Jn. 16:33). Paul and Barnabas said the same. They visited churches and reminded them: 'We must go through many hardships to enter the kingdom of God' (Acts 14:22). To put it bluntly, we'll have reasons aplenty to cry before we reach our heavenly home.

This isn't a cheerful message, I realise. But it's where the good news comes in.

We can be certain that no matter how bad, uncomfortable or undesirable our day is: God will be glorified. He has been glorified, and He will be glorified. How can we have this assurance? Romans 11:36 points us in the right direction: 'For from him and through him and for him are all things. To him be the glory for ever! Amen.'

Paul had just finished outlining the glories of redemption. That's the context. But the passage can be more widely applied.

'All things' doesn't *merely* refer to our salvation. 'All things' means *all* things. Everything. So, everything is from God, everything is through God and everything is for God.

All things in life are from, through and for Him. Even bad days. Even sleepless, baby-vomit-filled nights. Even fuzzy-headed, full days after those sleepless nights. All of it is from, to and through God – to the glory of His name. 'I am the Lord; that is my name! I will not yield my glory to another or my praise to idols' (Is. 42:8). However our day goes, God will not yield His glory to another. Every day works together to show how great God is, to raise our estimation of God and to lead us to praise His holy name. Every moment pulls in the same direction: God's glorious fame put on shining display. Doesn't this refocus our painful moments?

How does this work out in real time though? Lots of ways. I'm sleepy, but instead of being grumpy, I get on cleaning the bathroom, making my children lunch, reading my Bible, finishing that project for work and ringing my mum to check in on her. I'm exhausted, but with God's help, I just did what the day required. I fail an exam, but I don't let it consume me. I get on revising for the next exam two days later. God's glory is my goal in all things, whatever my exam results (1 Cor. 10:31). Or a bus hits a mucky puddle near the kerb of the pavement I'm walking on, and I'm sprayed with gritty water and left soaked. That's a bad day any way you slice it, isn't it? Yet even with my wet jeans and a meeting-filled day ahead, God is *still* glorified. Maybe He's glorified in some measure of perseverance I show though the strength He gives me (Phil. 4:13). We may not be able to join up all the dots, but God is glorifying Himself in *all* our circumstances. We want to always work with God for His glory, and repent quickly when we fail. But we must remember that God is glorified in all things.

Let me close with some specific counsel. When a bad day strikes, simplify things. Make it your goal, whatever your circumstances, to glorify God. Peter urges his readers this way, even amidst the persecution they faced:

> If anyone speaks, they should do so as one who speaks the very words of God. If anyone serves, they should do so with the strength God provides, so that in all things God may be praised through Jesus Christ. To him be the glory and the power for ever and ever (1 Pet. 4:11).

This counsel isn't trite. Peter himself knew suffering. This counsel can make our hard days, our sufferings, our persecution and even our sin more simple. God will be glorified today, whatever sort of day it is. This is a simple truth, and I pray it helps you. It helped and continues to help me.

Just to finish the story at the beginning: the baby did eventually fall asleep at about 4 AM. Mercifully, this gave me two hours of sleep before the other children awoke. Phew. I honestly can't remember how I handled the day. It's not as memorable as the night itself. Maybe it's not memorable because I just tried to do the best I could. But I do know, whatever I did, God glorified Himself. He always does and always will. That's the point, isn't it?

when sorrows like sea billows roll

23) Expectations

In the months following Megan's death, I had to drastically change my expectations for myself and our family. Before Megan's death, our family was busy with school, ministry, friendships, hobbies and holidays. Life was full. We were busy, but we felt like we were accomplishing observably good things. The shopping was done, a prison Bible study was led, school lessons were completed, friends had come round for food, that sermon was prepped, a key pastoral conversation was had, children had been disciplined, the washing up was done – the list could go on. Many nights, Megan and I would almost collapse into bed, but we were consoled by the fact that days felt both fruitful and productive.

This obvious productivity came to grinding halt with Megan's death. Imagine that for a moment. In a stroke, my life became about baby bottles. That's right: baby bottles. My days were filled with questions about them: Are they washed? Sterilised? Filled? At the right temperature? Sufficiently emptied? There was an orange bucket next to the kitchen sink, the repository of used bottles. The mountain of bottles in that bucket always seemed in need of a wash. So each night I washed them. And so the cycle went on. It's no exaggeration to say that I spent hours in those first six months just washing baby bottles. Sometimes

I cried as I washed them. Each washing session reminded me of Megan's death. That probably sounds weird. There were many other new priorities as well: nappies to change, meals to prep, a dog to walk, school runs to be made, finances to be re-tooled, children to be parented and a house to be looked after. I was doing stuff, but I didn't *feel* productive. Not like I had been before.

To be frank, most days felt futile. I wanted to do something big and important with my life. I wanted to help other people know, trust in and live for Jesus. This is a good goal, right? It was what God had kindly allowed us to do for years. And here I was doing nothing that seemed remotely related to that.

I can't lie: sometimes, anger creeped in. I don't want to try to justify it, and I'm ashamed to admit it. But I trust sharing this will help you. Ultimately, I had a heart issue. Jesus warns that out of our hearts (or our desires) come all sorts of trouble: "'What comes out of a person is what defiles them. For it is from within, out of a person's heart, that evil thoughts come … all these evils come from inside and defile a person'" (Mk. 7:20–23). Simply put, I wanted something different than what I had, and I was discontent and angry. I longed for the old productivity. I felt, even if I never said, 'I have skills and gifts, and I have seen the fruit of lives changed by the proclamation of God's Word. But now I am wasting all of this by merely washing baby bottles.'

It's sad, I know. Have you ever felt this way? Do you see something of this in yourself?

So what's the solution to discontentment and unrighteous anger? Spirit-empowered repentance.

As God exposed my heart and its strange fruit, that's what I sought to do: repent. The battle continues. Every day, I must replace desires and behaviour that don't please God with desires and behaviour that do (Eph. 4:20–24). Every day, my mind needs Scripture's renewal (Rom. 12:2). By God's grace, in those days, I began to fight this battle. I pursued Paul's contentment described: 'I have learned to be content whatever the circumstances' (Phil. 4:11). The 'secret' to contentment is to actively treasure Christ above all else (Phil. 3:7–8), and relying on His strength, to seek to please God whatever your circumstances. You really can be content through Him who gives you strength. So can I. I began, at least, to strain towards contentment.

Part of my repentance and my pursuit of contentment included recalibrating my expectations. I had to change my definition of a 'successful' or 'productive' day. It was a successful day if the baby had been fed, changed and put to bed. It was a successful day if the floor was swept and the bank account was still in the black. It was a productive day if I managed to get all the children to where they needed to be and in reasonably appropriate clothes. It was a *genuine* success if all of those baby bottles had been washed and were sitting ready for the next day's feedings!

'Success' was defined by whether I had been a good steward that day of the responsibilities God gave me. Have I taken the 'two bags of gold' I've been given and used, invested and grown them (Mt. 25:14–30)? Granted, sometimes what we have doesn't feel like two bags of gold, but have we taken whatever it is that God's given us and been faithful with it?

Our circumstances will change, often in ways we don't expect or want. So we must have this expectation as our baseline: 'Whatever comes today, I want to use well what God has given me.' We must pray: 'Lord, help me be a good steward.' We can (and should!) have grander goals and wisely work towards them, but faithful stewardship must always be our focus. The apostle Paul said: 'I eagerly *expect* and hope that I will in no way be ashamed, but will have sufficient courage so that now as always Christ will be exalted in my body, whether by life or by death' (Phil. 1:20, italics added). That's the sort of expectation recalibration we need.

I began writing a draft of this reflection during those first six months after Megan's death. In the middle of that draft, news broke that Joshua Harris (former pastor and writer of influential Christian books on dating) had separated from his wife and actually no longer identified as a Christian. I was gutted. Joshua Harris and his ministry had had a tremendous impact upon me for my spiritual good. But in God's funny providence, his apostasy had further shaped how I thought about expectations. I began to think: 'Any day where I don't curse Jesus and deny the gospel, that day is a success.' That may sound grim, but it's true. Christian, if the sun goes down and you still trust in Christ for your salvation, if you still love God and want to serve him – that day is a success. Whatever else happened that day, God has kept you. That's a good day.

Let's close this reflection with a few questions. Imagine for a moment that your life takes a sudden and drastic turn. You lose that job you really enjoy. Illness strikes leaving you bed-ridden for months. A family member has an accident, and you now are their full-time carer. Your wife dies.

When suffering like this strikes, your old plans and definitions of 'productivity' go out the window. How will you respond? Can you recalibrate your expectations and set your sights on faithful stewardship of whatever your life looks like *now*? These questions will be even harder to answer if you're a particularly 'successful' person in the world's eyes.

The eminent Reformed theologian BB Warfield is a powerful illustration for us. He refused the vast majority of invitations to speak across the USA and further abroad. Why? Warfield's wife, Annie, had a long-term health condition that left her almost completely housebound. Warfield felt unable to take any speaking engagement that forced him to be away from his wife. He was willing to forego the 'success' that speaking abroad might bring, and he was satisfied with the 'success' brought about by caring for his wife.

All of us must be a faithful steward of whatever God gives us. We just may, like Warfield, need to change our expectations.

when sorrows like sea billows roll

Section 3: The Longer Term

We'd managed to survive the first few months after Megan's death. So much, of course, had changed, as these pages have borne out. And so much more was yet to change. Still, though, our grief continued. At the same time, our grief also began to change. A year on, for example, we still missed Megan, but it felt less potent. Less immediate. Some memories had even started to fade. Photos bring the memories flooding back in, but time dims their intensity.

The reflections that follow round out the story of our family, and our longer term grief. There are unique lessons to be drawn from our sorrow even months and years on. I hope these chapters, as they conclude this purposeful memoir, will help you grieve well now and until Christ returns. There's a day coming when there will be no more grief. These reflections centre on all the days between today and that day. We need help to grieve well until the end.

when sorrows like sea billows roll

24) Beautiful places, an obvious absence, and a right sort of longing

Few places in all the world are more beautiful than Scotland. Almost seven months on from Megan's death, the children and I drove for 12½ hours to the home of friends on the edge of the Cairngorms near Aberdeen. We had been here a handful of times before, but every time we drive into the Highlands, I'm freshly gobsmacked. Such beauty. The children laugh at me because, as this drive draws to a close, I verbally exclaim (more than once) how beautiful Scotland is. I evoke groans as I inevitably say in a poor Scottish accent: 'This is loohve-lee.'

As beautiful as Scotland is, I find it hard coming to places that Megan and I both enjoyed together. And we *did* enjoy Scotland together. Family holidays, hill walks, river swims, cycle rides, bonfires, charity shop excursions, blaeberry picking (look it up!) and fried Mars bars – we enjoyed it all together!

That was then, and this is now. Today, it's like a pall hangs over my experience of this place *we* loved. A strange, dark fog. These places and experiences remind me of her, and I can't help but remember that she's not here now. Something's just missing that should be here.

This is the continued sadness that Megan's death brings about, even months and years on. Maybe this sensation will lessen or even go away one day? Some say it will. Others say that it never really goes away. That's hard.

I'm picking up this train of thought again a week into our Scottish holiday. It's been a wonderful week: the hospitality, the walks, the flowers blooming, the sweet Christian fellowship, and, yes, even the weather (I know, hard to believe isn't it?!). All of it has been brilliant. But still, Megan's not here. I've noticed her absence in all sorts of silly ways this last week. Let me explain one.

Ticks are nasty little blood-sucking insects. And they seem to enjoy Scotland as much as I do. Therefore, Scottish summers necessitate nightly tick checks. Before bed, you've got to give yourself a once over, or you can get into trouble fast. Although it's rare, a friend of mine got Lyme disease when one of these lovelies was left unchecked. It's going to sound strange, but even this simple routine of checking for ticks makes me miss Megan. I don't need to explain too much, but let's just say that Megan had been a help to me in the past. But she's not here to help now.

Whether or not there's marriage in the new heavens and new earth (Mt. 22:30) doesn't change the fact that Megan and I will one day 'do stuff' together again. I believe this. To make it even better, we will bow before the Lord Jesus together, see His face together, praise His holy name together and delightfully serve him for all eternity together. And we'll enjoy all of this with all our brothers and sisters in the faith. All of those redeemed by the grace of God will be there together. Megan and I will do stuff together again. That sounds so good.

As our trip to Scotland has drawn near, the children and I have been reading Randy Alcorn's book entitled *Heaven for Kids*. In a funny but heart-breaking twist, Megan actually bought this book for our family about a year before her death. Little did she know that when we would get round to reading it together, she would be there herself.

The children and I don't miss this funny fact for what it is: Megan continues to bless our family in so many ways, even beyond the grave. As we've read this book, I've been filled afresh with delight in and anticipation for the new heavens and new earth (Rev. 21–22). What a place that will be. Christ will appear, and all the created order will be turned on its head.

This helpful little book has reminded me of a truth that I reckon is forgotten by many Christians: the new heavens and new earth will be this very same heavens and earth, but reformed and renewed. Listen to 2 Peter 3:10–12:

> But the day of the Lord will come like a thief. The heavens will disappear with a roar; the elements will be destroyed by fire, and the earth and everything done in it will be laid bare. That day will bring about the destruction of the heavens by fire, and the elements will melt in the heat.

The earth as we know it now will be laid bare by fire. It'll be destroyed, but not in a total annihilation sort of way. More precisely, this earth will be cleansed by fire, and a new earth will come out of the purge. A renewed earth. 'Then I saw 'a new heaven and a new earth,' for the first heaven and the first earth had passed away, and there was no longer any sea' (Rev. 21:1). The old heaven and the old earth will be as good as dead, such will be the glory and fullness of the new. Think about that for a sec. What will that mean for you, Christian? It's hard to conceive of how great that place will be.

I knew this truth about the new heavens and the new earth, but Alcorn has meditated deeply on it. He's helped our family do the same. As we've done so, I've found that I really can't wait for it. I'm like a kid on Christmas morning, ready to come down the stairs and see what's under the tree. The presents will be unbelievable. I just know it. I know it may sound silly, but as I'm enjoying Scotland now I'm excited to explore 'New Scotland' on that day. Some of you may be rolling your eyes right now, but I don't think this is a stretch! Imagine Scotland, but free from all vestiges of the curse (like ticks?). All the fried Mars bars you could possibly want! Maybe Megan and I will get to see Scotland again, together, in the age to come?

Not seeing Megan here and now makes me long for that day so much more. From this perspective, perhaps the continued sadness is actually God's gift to me. Megan's absence helps me to long for heaven, which is supposed to be the way Christians live *everyday*. 'Instead, they were longing for a better country – a heavenly one. Therefore God is not ashamed to be called their God, for he has prepared a city for them' (Heb. 11:16).

As you feel similar pain and hardships under the sun, will you turn your heartache into a proper longing? If we train our hearts, sorrow and sadness now can lead us to long for and live for heaven that much more. A heaven where Scotland is even more beautiful than it is now. It's hard to imagine, but it's true.

when sorrows like sea billows roll

25) Still sovereign

The question plagued me: What *was* I going to do with the dog? Something had to be done. In a moment of passion during Megan's final days, I'd told the children: 'Whatever happens, we're keepin' the dog.' Yeah, about that. Months on and looking back, I became painfully aware that I'd made a valiant but foolhardy mistake. In my defence, wouldn't you do the same?

Think about it: how does a single dad of seven possibly look after a bouncy, fluffy white dog called Ridley? Didn't I have enough messes to clear up without having to sort his mucky, post-walk feet? On top of that, it just didn't feel fair to Ridley. All kidding aside, I could see it in his forlorn face. We weren't giving Ridley the exercise or the affection he needed. He clearly missed the high days of Megan. Seeing him low made me miss her that much more. So there I was. Stuck between the rock of my promise and the hard place of our inability to care for him. What *was* I going to do with the dog?

The issue of what to do with Ridley illustrates an important principle: as time passes, we face different problems. This seems simple enough, but hear me out. For most, a loved one's death leads to all sorts of immediate troubles. Funeral arrangements, emergency childcare, a reckoning with finances, and just getting through the day – all are pressing and painful realities. If you've made it this far, you've seen that many of these chapters have reflected on these sorts of problems. And I've tried to give biblical help to those in that place.

But eventually, the initial problems fade and new ones emerge. All the earlier problems don't get sorted perfectly, but people find themselves facing duller, maybe quieter, but no less painful problems months or years later.

Here, in no particular order, are some of the problems that hit me before and up to the first anniversary of Megan's death:

- My 8-year-old has another bad nosebleed, and I'm left to scrub blood out of the sofa
- It's getting late, dinner's still not on the table, and the 7-month-old is into the cupboards again
- It's Christmas Eve, and I am, for the first time ever and amidst tears, prepping Christmas dinner and, on my own, laying out our children's presents
- An error message pops up on the washing machine, and I have to clear out the vile-smelling filter or leave us without clean washing for another day
- My 14-year-old gets tonsillitis for the second time in six weeks, and no chemists are open to collect the prescription
- The children are desperate to keep Ridley, but keeping him, over time, seems more and more impossible.

I could go on, but here's the truth I want you to see: God was *still* sovereign. As He was in the big, tumultuous times of life, so He is in the small annoyances of life. And so He always will be. When that initial, intense period of problems gives way to new, more 'normal' problems, God is no less sovereign and no less good. His providence is no less total.

The Westminster Shorter Catechism (Question 11) defines providence this way: 'God's works of providence are his most holy, wise, and powerful preserving and governing all his creatures, and all their actions.' God wisely and powerfully preserves and governs *everything*. 'In the Lord's hand the king's heart is a stream of water that he channels towards all who please him' (Prov. 21:1). If the hearts of world rulers are in God's hands, I can be certain He's also sovereign in the nooks and crannies of my home and workplace, just as He was on the critical care ward. He sees and orchestrates nosebleeds and washer filters. He's providentially at work in all the new problems you face over time and every day. And He will be, whatever the future brings.

God's character and acts are consistent whatever the magnitude of our circumstances. As God was with His people at the edge of the Red Sea when grave disaster loomed (Ex. 14), so He was with His people in the wilderness when it seemed like food and water were scarce (Ex. 16–17). One problem might have felt 'big' and the other 'small,' but God was and is with His people always.

Here's a verse that has both vexed me and comforted me in recent years:

> For no one is cast off by the Lord for ever. Though he brings grief, he will show compassion, so great is his unfailing love.

> For he does not willingly bring affliction or grief to anyone (Lam. 3:31–33).

God does sovereignly bring grief, but he doesn't do so 'willingly.' What does this mean? I think it means the Lord brings grief with a compassionate heart and concern for the good of His people. You can take comfort here. God rules over all of your problems, He has not cast you off, and He's working for your good. 'And we know that in all things God works for the good of those who love him, who have been called according to his purpose' (Rom. 8:28). You need to be reminded of these truths when disaster strikes and when the the dull, quieter problems of life settle in.

I believe I'm unusual in this, but for me, it was easier to remember the sovereignty of God in the disastrous time around Megan's death. It sounds funny writing it here, but I usually think this way: 'Of course God's in control on the critical care ward, in the exam hall, at the crematorium or in the interview room!' I struggle, though, to believe that God is sovereign in the bedrooms, kitchens, classrooms, shops and offices. My faith may seem great in the whirlwind of the big moment, but I fall into anger, discontentment and worry in the 'small' problems of life. It seems counterintuitive, but it's how I often struggle.

But we must think well in the big and the small. We must train ourselves to see God's kind, providential care. If we're watching (or maybe better, believing), God's provision can be seen everywhere. Let me testify to God's goodness on behalf of our family. I listed some of our problems earlier, but let me couple them with God's equally pleasant providences from the same period:

- Two different sets of friends flew over (at their own expense) to help us with a few big, practical needs round the house. One group organised our overwhelming stock of children's clothes. The other group constructed our garden sheds. Both encouraged us with their fellowship
- Our 3-year-old was offered a nursery spot practically before I had even asked
- I discovered I had skin cancer and had it surgically removed without too much fanfare
- All eight of us (plus a family friend to help with childcare!) travelled across the Atlantic to my sister's wedding six months on from Megan's death. It was a fun and restful time away
- The baby, remarkably, continued to gain weight and grow (despite my parenting)!
- In the summer, we were able to have a beautiful week's worth of camping in Kent (the garden of England!) before the school year began again in full
- Our church family and other local pastor friends continued to provide for us and check in on me regularly.

Maybe you're a few months or a few years on from tragedy. Time has passed, but the pain and related problems persist. Don't lose sight of God's providence. Whether our troubles seem big or small. God is fulfilling His purpose for you. 'I cry out to God Most High, to God who fulfils his purpose for me' (Ps.

57:2, ESV). Rest in this. Rejoice in this. And repent quickly where needed. I needed to repent regularly of my discontentment, anger and unbelief. As I did, 1 John 1:9 comforted me: 'If we confess our sins, he is faithful and just and will forgive us our sins and purify us from all unrighteousness.'

So, God is still sovereign. Over all. Even our dog, Ridley. Well, I guess he's our former dog for now. In God's kindness, without me asking, some good friends in Kent offered to 'foster' Ridley for us. Oh, he'd still be 'our' dog, and we could see him whenever we liked. But our friends would look after Ridley indefinitely. They were happy to have him for two years or the rest of his life. But anytime we wanted him back, he'd be ours. Can you think of a better arrangement than this?

At time of writing, Ridley's been living the country life in rural Kent for almost three years. He loves his daily walks along the bridal paths of Kent, and he does so as a testament to God's sovereign care of me and our family. Do you have eyes to see such care in your life?

26) Everybody hurts, everybody cries ... sometimes

I didn't cry at Megan's funeral or her graveside service. I wore the same blue suit to both. I smiled and even laughed at both services and during the teas that followed. I don't know how you're supposed to act at your wife's funeral. Over the next few months, I got on looking after the children, did the school run, gave haircuts and tried to get back to work. I did the shopping, prepared meals, and even started having people into our home for meals again. Through it all, I grieved and got on each day as best I could.

And for a lot of that period, I smiled. Sometimes I didn't. I also don't know how you're supposed to act eight months after your wife dies. On the first anniversary of Megan's death, I received so many kind messages. I replied, I think, to all of them. Around that same time, we had a full house for what used to be our annual New Year's Eve open house. I made chilli, we had pineapple upside down cake, we made jokes, and we generally enjoyed the evening. Of course, it was tinged with sadness so near to the anniversary of Megan's death. Believe it or not, I also don't know how you're supposed to behave around the first anniversary of your wife's death. Cry? Laugh? Be sombre? Smile? All of the above?

I'm not sure there *is* a way you're supposed to behave. At that time, an obvious truth began to dawn on me: everybody grieves differently. Over the course of that first year, I saw this truth as I interacted with other people who themselves were grieving Megan's death.

Let me give you three composite reactions to Megan's death, each drawn from actual interactions.

> **Reaction 1:** 'Brad, you look tired. I'd be the same way. You're doing well though. Keep it up.'
>
> **Reaction 2:** 'I don't know how you made it through the funeral. I would have been crying my eyes out. I still would be.'
>
> **Reaction 3:** 'You must be missing Megan so much [awkward pause to regain composure]. Her death reminds me of my brother's tragic death.'

Of course, I'm not classifying any of these as right or wrong. Just notice: they're all slightly different.

The Bible contains a diverse sample of grievers. Let's see three.

First, David. He's under threat, and he cries to the Lord. He prays for retribution to fall on his enemies. Yet when his enemies themselves are near death, David describes how he felt: 'Yet when they were ill, I put on sackcloth and humbled myself with fasting. When my prayers returned to me unanswered, I went about mourning as though for my friend or brother. I bowed my head in grief as though weeping for my mother' (Ps. 35:13–14).

Next, consider Nehemiah. From Susa, he hears of the fate of the Israelites still living in Israel and the sorry state of Jerusalem's walls. Nehemiah's reaction: 'When I heard these things, I sat down and wept. For some days I mourned and fasted and prayed before the God of heaven' (Neh. 1:4). Then, he moves to rectify the situation.

Lastly, consider Jesus. Upon Lazarus's death, many weep at the tomb. Then the onlookers recognise, in Jesus's tears, His love for Lazarus (Jn. 11:36). You probably know how this ends: Lazarus is miraculously raised to life.

So, in sum, Nehemiah grieved for his homeland and people, and he got busy. David grieved at his enemies' plight, just as he'd weep for his mum. Then he captured his grief in poetry. Jesus weeps. Yet a resurrection transforms the scene from sorrow to joy. Three different grievers. For three different reasons. Leading to three different reactions.

Anecdotal evidence urges me to push my point one step further: everybody grieves differently AND most people expect you to grieve like they do. We don't do this intentionally. But think about it: we're surprised when someone cries, and we barely felt a flicker of emotion. We're taken aback when someone doesn't sob, when our eyes are splotchy and red with tears. We see it in the questions we ask ourselves: 'Have I got this wrong? Am I just overly emotional? Does she not have a heart?' We compare ourselves to others and their reactions. We may even, in our worst moments, be offended or hurt if others don't feel or act the way we do. As others grieved Megan's death differently than me, I began to ask a weird questions: 'Do people think, because I don't cry like they do, that I didn't love Megan? Because I did, and I do! I may not cry much, but don't think that means I don't miss her!' I felt compelled to express my love for Megan out loud to others, just to prove that I loved her! Like I said: different grievers, different reasons, different reactions and even different expectations.

What should we do about this? Let's remember what Hebrews 13:3 tells us: 'Continue to remember those in prison as if you were together with them in prison, and those who are ill-treated as if you yourselves were suffering.' We need to actively think of and care for brothers and sisters who are in a bad way. We need to identify with them, as if their suffering were our own.

Because, well, it is.

'If one part suffers, every part suffers with it; if one part is honoured, every part rejoices with it' (1 Cor. 12:26). Such is our unity with other Christians, *especially* within our local church. Your redundancy is my redundancy. Your rebellious child breaks my heart, too. Your new flat purchase near the church is a win for me, even if I'm still in a bedsit a couple miles away. I'm to think of your ups and downs as mine, and care for you as best I can according to your needs.

Paul echoes this admonition in Romans 12:15: 'Rejoice with those who rejoice; mourn with those who mourn.' We're to actively celebrate other's successes and grieve over their sorrows. This is a command to feel with others, in so far as we can, or at a minimum, it's a command to be aware of others' joys and sorrows and treat them fittingly. I may not have a miscarriage, but your miscarriage affects me too. Inversely, your award of recognition at work is a cause for shared celebration. If you're happy, I'm happy. If you're hurting, I'm hurting. My aim: to know you, your ailments, and your normal way of grieving so that I might love and serve you in your sorrows. Peter sums up well the Christian's responsibility to grievers: 'Finally, all of you, be like-minded, be sympathetic, love one another, be compassionate and humble' (1 Pet. 3:8).

Let's summarise all that we've said so far, and make a final appeal. Christians, recognise that your brothers and sisters don't grieve like you do. So don't hold them to your standard of grieving. Be humble, patient and sympathetic in your dealings with each other. Your goal is to 'please God' (2 Cor. 5:9), not look exactly like others.

Let me close by offering a two-part appeal. First, Christians: get to know your brothers and sisters well. Be a committed member of your church. Get extensive time, socially (think food and drink!), with other members. Do stuff together. And as you do, ask questions about each other's highs and lows. Pay attention to where you can help when the time comes. Then, praying for help, do it. Second, if you're an elder of a church, encourage this kind of culture in your church. Does your sermon application direct the church in how to care for each other in times of suffering? Are you modelling this kind of awareness and mutual care in your personal life and in your ministry to the flock (1 Pet. 5:2–3)? May the Lord help us here to His glory and our good.

I'm still not sure how to act at your wife's funeral. Or at the one-year or three-year anniversary of her death. I look back and ask myself: 'Did I handle that well?' And I don't have an answer! But this much I do know: I loved my wife. I miss her like crazy. I smiled. Sometimes I cried. I still do. I'm okay with that.

27) Waging war

Here's a warning up front: this reflection was awkward to write, and it'll probably be awkward to read. Especially if you're English. Nonetheless, I reckon a chapter on sex and the widower is needed. There's no getting round it: from the moment Megan died, I faced sexual temptation. How was I to respond? And how might you respond to sexual temptation in your life, perhaps particularly while you're grieving? Let me try to use my situation to encourage you.

First, I want to describe my situation but through a different lens. When Megan died, I'd only just turned 38 years old. Young, right? As I write this, I'm 40. Still young! My children dispute that claim, but never mind. Back to the point: Megan and I had been married 14 years at the time of her death. We were both virgins on our wedding day and, due to God's generosity, we enjoyed a consistent sexual relationship throughout our married life. You can do the maths: God gave us seven children together. Praise God for His kindness in these things.

Some were losing a daughter, mother, sister or friend. I was losing a wife and a lover. I was losing one who knew me more intimately than any other, one with whom I had been naked and felt 'no shame' (Gen. 2:25). As we turned off life-support, it

161

dawned on me that Megan and I would never again share our bodies.

So it was. Gone were the cuddles, the kisses, the tender touches and, of course, our sexual relationship. Almost overnight, our physical interactions of 14 years were cut off. When Megan died, I tangibly missed her body. As many know, the physical relationship with your spouse is meant to be a comfort, an encouragement and a pleasure. Megan's death revoked all of that. I was, yet again, a single man. And sex was suddenly off-limits.

I feel crass describing some of my thoughts from the time. 'Were you really thinking about this around Megan's death? I mean, how unfeeling can you be?' The answers: yes, I was. And, I guess, very. As we buried Megan in a churchyard in Kent, my heart ached. I missed Megan in every way including physically. I know this is not a unique experience.

At that time, I sensed that a battle loomed. A battle different from any I'd faced before. I'd tasted the good fruit of a married sexual relationship. Now, I had to live a pure life, pleasing to God in every way. Peter urges believers, 'Abstain from sinful desires, which wage war against your soul' (1 Pet. 2:11). Our sinful desires wage war against our souls. It's life or death, and we have to learn how to fight back.

Here's where I want to encourage you. I want to offer you four tips I learnt along the way.

Tip 1: Remember the promises of God.

Christian, the old you that was enslaved to sin died when Jesus died, and the new you that is free to obey God began with Jesus' resurrection (Rom. 6:11–14). You no longer *have* to give in to sin. You're cleansed from sin and free to live a life pleasing to God (1 Cor. 6:11). This positional reality cannot be overstated when faced with sinful desire. *Who* you are shapes *how* you fight the battle.

Two other promises particularly helped me. First, John 13:17 says, 'Now that you know these things, you will be blessed if you do them.' Jesus reminds His disciples that blessing follows obedience. In the immediate context, He's talking about sacrificial service that leads to blessing. But the principle can be more widely applied. We *think* that blessing (or happiness) comes from sinful gratification. Jesus says the opposite. Do you *really* want happiness? If so, do what God says.

Second, Jesus promises that those with pure hearts will see God (Mt. 5:8). Think about that: those who live purely will see all the splendour of God one day. To see God will be an undiluted delight. Which pleasure is most compelling to you? Happiness and seeing God one day, or sexual gratification today?

Tip 2: Practice good, old self-control.

Scripture doesn't mince words in its instruction to those tempted by sexual sin: 'Flee!' (1 Cor. 6:18–20). 'Be sanctified ... avoid sexual immorality ... learn to control your own body in a way that is holy and honourable, not in passionate lust like the pagans, who do not know God' (1 Thes. 4:3–5).

Today, I fear we read these commands, and we chuckle. As if to say: 'We know we can't really do that, so why try?' Or maybe: 'That sounds so legalistic.' Oh, if we talk this way, how far we've fallen from the tree of biblical Christianity! But the command is explicit and powerful: run away from sexual immorality. Say 'no' to yourself and 'no' to any sexual desire, experience or relationship that doesn't take place within the friendly, blessed confines of a heterosexual marriage. Say 'no' to incest, pornography, masturbation, sodomy, adultery and fornication. We need these exhortations. The battle, humanly speaking, depends on your ability to discipline yourself and say 'no' to your desires. It was clear where I would struggle as an unmarried man, but it was equally clear how I was meant to behave. Thankfully, no Christian need 'muscle up' the power to please God on his or her own. 'God works in you to will and to act in order to fulfil his good purpose' (Phil. 2:13). The same power that raised Jesus from the dead is in us to help us live unto God.

This is where the battle often takes place. It did for me. I wanted sexual gratification. I had to act carefully in my interactions with attractive women. I had to think twice about my entertainment (and maybe more carefully than ever as I lacked a God-given sexual outlet). To make this clear: watching a film with any sort of suggestive activity or nudity was well out of bounds because sexual desires instigated had nowhere to go! At other times, I had to be open about my battle with my brothers in Christ. I spoke occasionally with a number of men about the battle and my temptations. Hardest of all: I had to say 'no' in moments of private temptation. You know the ones I mean. In my room at night, on my own, I had to use my phone well. 'Nobody' else was there. It's these kinds of places where the battle raged for me. The call: self-control, spurred on by God's help.

Tip 3: Throw yourself headlong into local church life.

This is perhaps the most neglected 'help' when Christians talk about standing firm in the face of sexual temptation. Those who throw themselves into their local church are best equipped to fight the battle with sexual temptation. They have 'brothers in arms,' and they're equipped for the daily battle.

> And let us consider how we may spur one another on towards love and good deeds, not giving up meeting together, as some are in the habit of doing, but encouraging one another – and all the more as you see the Day approaching (Heb. 10:24–25).

Think about those verses in light of sexual temptation. My counsel: be at church for the morning and evening services. Listen well to the preached Word. Pray fervently with and for the church family. Regularly take the Lord's Supper. Serve the body, especially doing the 'menial tasks' the church needs you to do in order for it to function. Check in on the elderly. Babysit for the young families. Share meaningful conversation over meals and coffee. Be open about your temptations with your elders and seek their help in the fight. In sum, simply be involved body and soul in the fellowship of your church family. Be all in. Few things helped me more in my battle with sexual temptation. I needed the church. You need the church, too.

165

If your current church doesn't have the sort of fellowship or accountability I'm describing here, can you help to foster it?

Tip 4: Get married.

So many rubbish this solution today. 'Tut tut,' they say, 'Doesn't he know that being married doesn't stop sexual sin (let alone sexual temptation!).' [Insert here a condescending laugh directed at nubes like me.]

Well, of course being married doesn't *solve* your sexual sin problems! In fact, it kinda creates some new ones. But marriage, undeniably, is the biblically prescribed solution to sexual desire. To paraphrase Paul's message: 'If you burn, get married' (1 Cor. 7:1–9).

If you have sexual desire at all, there is only one acceptable output for that desire: heterosexual marriage. As such, I knew that the only place my sexual desire could be legitimately gratified. I had to get married. Or, in my case, remarried. I'll return to the topic of remarriage in a later chapter. But for now, know that remarriage was another weapon in my 'arsenal' as I waged war with sexual temptation. Have you considered that weapon in your case?

I hope these tips help you. Let me put a bow on this by telling you how things have gone for me. I hate it when stories don't provide any hint of a conclusion, so let me try. Of course, my battle with temptation is not finished yet, but looking back, I definitely 'burned' (in the 1 Corinthians 7 sense) especially early on after Megan's death. But the fact is that God graciously

166

'turned down' those pressing desires during that time. It was as if the 'tap' of my sexual desires was turned right down to a trickle. Oh, the desires were still there, but in the absence of legitimate output, they were kindly muted. This was a gift from God. And I assume it will not necessarily be the case for everyone. I can testify, with a clear conscience, that God has kept me sexually pure. All praise to him. Let this encourage you, whatever your situation or your failures. Press on to purity today, even as I too need to keep pressing on to purity.

Behind my desk on my bookshelf, right now, is a booklet. It was written by a pastor who, after writing the booklet, made shipwreck of his life and ministry by giving way to sexual sin. This booklet sits there as a haunting reminder for me. Let us never let down our guard. We must wage war until Jesus returns or He calls us home.

when sorrows like sea billows roll

28) A secure fortress for us and a refuge for our children

Children say some funny things. Sometime after Megan's death, a precocious 4-year-old in our church said to me: 'Megan's dead. My grandad's dead.' That was, no joke, how the conversation began. And apparently, it was all he wanted to say! Gut-wrenching, right? And yet strangely hilarious. I wasn't sure if I should laugh or cry.

Thankfully, I had a pre-packaged response for awkward moments like this one: 'That's right. Megan is dead. Do *you* know where she is now?' And off we went to a brief chat about heaven and how we get there through Jesus's death and resurrection. I mention this conversation because it pictures something we know: children think about death. Of course, they struggle to understand and respond (politely or otherwise!). But they feel it no less painfully than adults. Death hurts us all.

I can't tell you how many times I've been asked the same question since Megan's death: 'How are the *children* doing?' I appreciate being asked. The question shows concern for me and for the children. The trouble is: I often struggle to answer it. Why? Because I have 7 children! All of them grieve differently. Some have been more tearful; some haven't shed a drop. One seems to think about Megan regularly, asking questions about what she liked or disliked. Others don't externally miss her, even if they internally do. Some children have been openly angry about Megan's death and the knock-on effects it's had on our family. Others have soldiered on quietly. To repeat myself: no two people (including children) grieve in the same way. Which makes it hard to report how my children are doing!

I can give anecdotes of course. Here are two. Not long after Megan's death, one of the younger children asked when we were going to go and collect mummy from heaven. That one almost broke me. This sort of question came up regularly in the early days.

On another occasion, many months after Megan's death, we were enjoying 'just one more' hug before bed, when a child started sobbing. When I queried the tears (guessing their origin), this child pointed with their toe to a photo of Megan next to the bed. That 'one more' hug became something of an extended cuddle. It was sweet and yet heart-breaking.

Though often unseen, the children's grief was certainly there. We've done our best to be aware of it, lovingly interact with it and grow through it. How are they doing though? Sometimes alright, sometimes not. A bit like all of us.

So how do we respond to children's grief? If we're in a position to care for children, we need biblical guidance.

As I've seen my own children grieve, a few patterns have emerged. And if the Bible does have what we need for life and godliness (2 Pet. 1:3), we ought to see what it says about these patterns.

Let me make a few preliminary observations about children's grief learned from our experience, and then I'll follow that up with some key biblical truths and follow-on counsel. I am drawing heavily from the book of Proverbs because it's tailored to helping young people grow in wisdom in all areas of life, which of course includes their grief.

The observations:

Firstly, sorrow can pop up at absolutely any time. It's hard to tell when and where a child may experience grief. This seems simplistic, but it's important. For us, family meals and bedtime have often prompted reflection and sadness. And I don't think it's merely my cooking or a ploy to stay up past bedtime! For whatever reason, those times foster reminiscing, and so we've all missed Megan. But grief has also hit us at unexpected times. Be aware.

Secondly, children rarely understand the magnitude of death. To say it in a silly way: death's a 'game changer.' Relationships and routines (realities so important to children) – death alters these and more. To put it mildly, this is sad and hard. Children need comfort and assistance to navigate the emotions and shifting practicalities death brings.

Thirdly, your child's grief and their response to it will be (for better or worse) shaped by your grief and your response to it. I've seen this in many ways. My children have reflected me. It's scary but true.

None of these observations are particularly novel. But they do provide the typical context into which the Bible speaks and directs.

So, what *does* the Bible say?

First, recognise it's not a sin to be sad.

This bears repeating. The obvious example: Jesus experienced loss and was sad (Jn. 11:35). So too will our children. And though being sad is not sin, it is sin to disobey God's Word in response to sad things. Sinful anger or sinful discouragement, worry or fear – these responses to grief don't please God. 'Refrain from anger and turn from wrath; do not fret – it leads only to evil' (Ps. 37:8). We must train ourselves and our children to glorify God in and through our grief.

Second, the Lord Jesus Christ is our blessed and only hope (Tit. 2:13).

There is hope 'held out in the gospel' (Col. 1:23) for sad people. Though we're sad, Christians anticipate a sorrow-free eternity because Jesus died and rose again redeeming sinners like us. 'Like cold water to a weary soul is good news from a distant land' (Prov. 25:25). This is not 'pie in the sky' thinking: the gospel brings real comfort to real and sad people. Our children need this hope repeated again and again.

Third, laughter and sadness can go together.

'Even in laughter the heart may ache, and rejoicing may end in grief' (Prov. 14:13). Our emotional lives are jumbled. And this intermixing can be weird and yet comforting. We must leverage this in our parenting through grief. It's good and it's okay to laugh. And to cry.

Fourth, parents must trust God and continue parenting.

'Start children off on the way they should go, and even when they are old they will not turn from it' (Prov. 22:6). There's a common fear that pervades Christian families who experience death. They're afraid that as a result of their loss, the children will grow up angry and, in turn, reject God. This fear is not ungrounded, and it sometimes cripples grieving families. Acknowledging this reality helps us, but we must trust God and continue to 'bring them up in the training and instruction of the Lord' (Eph. 6:4).

Finally, Christian parents must cry out to God for wisdom.

None of us knows how to handle every personality and circumstance surrounding death and grief. But Scripture promises the Lord will help us and our children: 'Whoever fears the Lord has a secure fortress, and for their children it will be a refuge' (Prov. 14:26). Fear the Lord, call out to Him for help and anticipate God meeting your needs and then some.

These truths are, from one vantage point, so simple! But we forget them in our grief. But they help us as we help the children in our lives. Building upon the common observations and the Bible's truths, let's draw out some closing biblical counsel in no particular order:

Create time or give time for talking about how your child is doing.

Even the most secular book on grief will say this, but it's good counsel. We must listen and then speak, and be careful not to reverse the order: 'To answer before listening – that is folly

173

and shame' (Prov. 18:13). It is only as we hear from our children, probing their hearts through their mouths (Mt. 12:34), that we'll be able to speak words of encouragement, comfort and direction. 'The soothing tongue is a tree of life' (Prov. 15:4). I want to have this sort of tongue, but it begins by making time for listening.

When your children do bring up their sorrows, slow things down and linger there.

It takes time to draw out the purposes of your children's hearts. Their hearts are deep. 'The purposes of a person's heart are deep waters, but one who has insight draws them out' (Prov. 20:5). You'd do well to ask questions in order to draw them out more. What are they thinking? What do they miss and why? What do they want to do about it all? Careful listeners make the best witnesses (Prov. 21:28), so too will your unhurried listening prompt wise parenting. As a side note, lingering often opens up times for laughter and thankful remembrance. 'Remember when your mummy used to' has been a constant source of laughter for us, even amidst sorrow. The key: slowing down.

Don't lie about hard realities, but share them with children in an age-appropriate and time-sensitive way.

I know parents who refused to use the word 'dead' with children to describe their deceased parent. Of course, we have to be thoughtful here, but lying or hiding harsh truths rarely helps. 'The words of the reckless pierce like swords, but the tongue of the wise brings healing' (Prov. 12:18). Fear the Lord, pray for wisdom and speak. Truthfully. 'A truthful witness saves lives,' and 'An honest answer is like a kiss on the lips' (Prov. 14:25; 24:26). Our children knew, often within minutes or hours, the harsh realities of Megan's decline and death. I believe they were better for it. The truth hurt, but it gave the opportunity for hope-filled healing.

Admit your own struggles and be intentional in sharing your grief.

You're grieving, too. Why would you hide this from your children? Do you want to appear strong? There can be a place for bravery, but there's also a place for sharing your pain and pointing to the hope that persists amidst the pain. 'Gracious words are a honeycomb, sweet to the soul and healing to the bones' (Prov. 16:24). That's what you want, isn't it? I've found with my children that sharing how I miss Megan has been fertile ground to reflect on the grace of God in Christ. The shared experience of sorrow can lead to shared hope and joy.

Lean into godly fellowship for yourself and for the children.

One of the greatest helps to our children's grief has been our loving church family. Proverbs 17:17 says, 'A friend loves at all times, and a brother is born for a time of adversity.' Our brothers and sisters have just, frankly, been there – being kind, providing for our needs, speaking truth to us and encouraging us by their persevering faith in Christ. They've loved Jesus and loved us. My children have seen this, and they love our church for it. They really have. Few comforts have been more felt. If you don't have this sort of Christian fellowship now, search for a good church and settle there today. There are lots of reasons to do so, but if anything, do so for your children's future sorrows. The local church helps us grieve well and comforts us in our grief.

Our children need us to help them grieve well. Hopefully these biblical truths and tidbits of counsel help you help the little ones in your life.

29) Mr Optimism

I am a 'glass half full' sort of guy. My friends might call me an optimist. I admit it. I *do* usually think things are going to work out just fine. And even if they don't, and everything does go pear-shaped, well, that'll be just fine too, won't it?

True to form, I usually feel pretty happy about my optimism. I mean, what's not to like? Well, about a year on from Megan's death, I had a conversation that caused me to re-think my optimism due to its possible effect on others. I can boil the conversation down to one comment. Over a pulled pork sandwich, my friend Andrew said, 'If anybody could handle this sort of trial, it'd be you, Brad. You're so optimistic.'

He said this to encourage me, and it did. This was how he praised God for carrying us through this trial. At the same time, this comment troubled me. Why?

Firstly, because all Christians have a hard time grieving well, and this discourages us. We worry. We get depressed. Frankly, we just don't know how to cope. We want to be calm, cool, and collected under fire, but we're not. I want to share the gospel with my neighbour when he asks how I'm coping, but I rarely do. We feel like we crawl through hardship.

His comment troubled me because I worry that Christians wonder if their personality was just different, then this wouldn't be so hard for them. 'If I wasn't a pessimist, or if I was just 'Type A,' or if I was just more expressive, then I would be doing so much better.'

But here's the problem: if our response to suffering hangs on our personalities, then we're in trouble. Our hope for glorifying God in our trials isn't dependent on my so-called optimism.

Now, I know Andrew didn't intend this, but you can see how someone might slip into this sort of thinking. His comment troubled me because I want to give all Christians hope for pleasing God in suffering – whatever their personality type! If my optimism inadvertently robs people of hope, then maybe I need to be a bit quieter with it.

This kind of thinking can show up in lots of ways:

- 'I have a nervous disposition, so I can't help but worry about my finances. I mean, energy prices just keep going up'
- 'I blew up at my dad again. I always get so angry when he won't let me go out with my friends. There's no hope for me. I don't want to get angry, but I always do'
- 'I want to be married, but I'm so shy. I get so anxious whenever a relationship seems to be picking up steam. I feel so stuck'
- 'I'm just a melancholic person. When I'm feeling low, I struggle to get to church'
- 'My husband has died, and I just don't see a way out of this situation. The children, the finances – everything just seems a mess. I'm sure others wouldn't struggle as I do, but I can't see a way out'

Do you hear yourself in any of these? We may never say this explicitly, but we often do feel *bound* by our personality.

God has, of course, crafted us with a unique make up of likes, dislikes, outlooks on life, leanings and tendencies – in other words, with unique personalities. So how do we, as the people we are, deal with suffering? How should I respond if I get cancer, or lose my job? If we have another miscarriage? If the stock market dip means my pension is slashed? If war breaks out or my wife unexpectedly dies?

With our specific personalities, how can we glorify God in these situations?

Let me offer three answers. Humanly speaking, Christians suffer well if:

They know the truth.

They have thought through and recognised the importance of truths like God's fatherly care, Christ's redeeming work and continued intercession, the Holy Spirit's indwelling work, the Christian's hope of eternity in God's presence, and Scripture's sufficiency. This list could go on without end. I'm writing this book, in part, to help Christians know some of these truths and connect them to their suffering. It's unarguable: if you find a Christian who suffers to the glory of God, then you will find a Christian who knows and loves these truths.

They know their personality.

Our natural leanings shape our response to trials. After Megan's death, my personality drove me forward. I wanted to solve the problems before us, I wanted to not be overwhelmed, and I wanted to be sure that it would all work out. Others would have responded differently. They would simply feel less capable. They would be unable to see a way forward, and they would struggle to believe things will work out. Our nervous dispositions, shy temperaments, and general outlooks on life do have an impact! A key to suffering well is being aware of how you tick. Calvin said, 'Nearly all the wisdom we possess, that is to say, true and sound wisdom, consists in two parts: the knowledge of God and of ourselves.' Unless we know God and unless we know ourselves, we will not be wise and we will not glorify God in suffering.

They discipline their thinking according to Scripture.

If you're going to suffer well, then you must match up your personality to the truth. Think about it. You must believe the truths you're particularly prone to forget. You must remind yourself of the truths you believe, though your experience, feelings, and natural predisposition tells you otherwise. Simply put, your self-awareness must be guided by the Bible. You must learn to say 'no' to your feelings or personality and 'yes' to the truth. This is what it looks like to live in such a way as to 'please God' (2 Cor. 5:9) whatever your circumstances.

In Romans 12:2, the Apostle Paul says, 'Do not conform to the pattern of this world, but be transformed by the renewing of your mind.' To have our minds 'renewed' is to think more biblically about God, ourselves and our circumstances. To 'renew your mind' is to think as God thinks and process life through the lens of His Word. It's what Paul described as both the one-time *and* the continual experience of the Ephesians: 'You were taught, with regard to your former way of life, to put off your old self, which is being corrupted by its deceitful desires; to be made new in the attitude of your minds' (Eph. 4:22–23). They'd been taught this, it had happened in part, but the Ephesians (and all Christians) must be made new in the attitude of the minds.

This is the point, in part, of Psalm 119. This majestic (and long!) psalm is often seen as a reflection on the Scriptures. It certainly is that, but if you read closely, you'll see that the psalmist is suffering.[18] Particularly, he's facing persecution for his commitment to the Lord. How does he deal with his struggles? He has disciplined his thinking.

- Verse 15 – 'I meditate on your precepts and consider your ways.' Where is the Psalmist's mind focused? This sort of statement appears all over Psalm 119

- Verse 28 – 'My soul is weary with sorrow; strengthen me according to your word.' Do you get a sense of his circumstances? We don't know the nature of his wearying sorrow, but he knows his strength both spiritually and physically comes from God's Word. His experience is countered and directed by the Bible

- Verses 67–68 – 'Before I was afflicted I went astray, but now I obey your word. You are good, and what you do is

---

18 David Powlison first helped me see Psalm 119 this way. For a fuller (and more helpful!) analysis of this Psalm, read 'Suffering and Psalm 119' in *Speaking the Truth in Love: Counsel in Community*, New Growth Press, 2005.

good; teach me your decrees.' His affliction has had at least one positive outcome: it has led him to obey God's Word. He has seen the goodness of God more clearly. In suffering, the truth met his personality, and he glorified God

- Verses 82–83 – 'My eyes fail, looking for your promise; I say, 'When will you comfort me?' Though I am like a wineskin in the smoke, I do not forget your decrees.' How vivid is his language here! He might have been classified as a pessimist, yet he doesn't forget God's decrees

- Verse 143 – 'Trouble and distress have come upon me, but your commands give me delight.' God's commands are his 'delight' even amidst distress and trouble

- Verse 165 – 'Great peace have those who love your law, and nothing can make them stumble.' How can he say this amid such opposition and suffering? He's disciplined his mind to believe the truth. He may or may not be an optimist, but his mind is being renewed.

Whatever your personality, be hopeful when troubles strike! The Psalmist teaches us how to think about our losses, illnesses, headaches, A&E trips, job losses, utility bill spikes, burnt dinners, and family conflicts. We should view our circumstances (and our personality) through the lens of the Bible. God's promises, laws, commands and decrees must be our delight, direction, strength and comfort.

Let me close this reflection with one important question for you: What sort of personality do you have? What are your tendencies when hardships come upon you? If you don't know, ask a mature Christian who knows you well.

when sorrows like sea billows roll

30) A crown

Weddings are usually a joy for all involved. Who isn't delighted to see two become one at that most solemn and merry of occasions? Well, if I'm totally honest, I was, and I wasn't. Let me explain. I was positively torn at the first wedding I attended after Megan's death. Rejoicing in God's goodness to the young couple? Absolutely. Honoured to preach God's Word and proclaim the gospel to all gathered? Certainly. Missing Megan like crazy? Yep. Wishing Megan were there with me during the meal and other activities that followed? More than I can put into words.

Weddings for widows can be painful. At that first wedding, I really noticed Megan's absence. At weddings, couples often stay near to each other. In a potentially awkward social setting, your spouse gives you an easy conversation partner! For me, that support was gone. I wanted my wife, and she wasn't there.

I missed Megan in another way that day though. Whilst Megan and I were married, it was always a thrill to attend weddings. Seeing another man and woman join their lives always seemed to revive our appreciation for the gift of marriage. It was like: 'Oh yeah, this thing we have, this marriage, it really is a great gift from God.' What Christian isn't delighted to be reminded of this glorious picture of Christ's love for His church? So, I *was* thrilled that day, but I was also filled with sorrow.

I had this social support. I had this gift. I had this glorious picture in our marriage. But not anymore.

Now, before you start to think this is going to be one long moan, let me cut to the chase. Being at that wedding that day made one thing clear to me: I wanted to be married again. It's okay to say that, isn't it? Maybe it's just my impression, but I feel like there's a bit of social awkwardness around remarriage. It's awkward because remarriage means a mixing of our sorrow over the death of a spouse and our happiness with the thought of a new relationship. It's awkward because remarriage affects so many people, especially when there are kids involved. So it's a topic to be handled with care and proceeded into with caution.

Now, let's open the 'can of worms' that is remarriage. Let me get at this by asking five key questions and then offer biblical answers to each. I'm asking these questions from the perspective of a widow or widower, but hopefully the general reader can reappropriate them appropriately.

Question One: 'Should I get remarried?'

If your spouse has died, there is no quibbling with the biblical answer: widows and widowers are 'free' to remarry. 'A woman is bound to her husband as long as he lives. But if her husband dies, she is free to marry anyone she wishes, but he must belong to the Lord' (1 Cor. 7:39) To remarry, upon the death of a spouse, is permitted.

Now, this is categorically a different question to whether you *should* get remarried. One must be careful about whom they marry. One's happiness (not to mention one's spiritual health) is tied up with whom you marry: 'A wife of noble character is her husband's crown, but a disgraceful wife is like decay in his bones' (Prov. 12:4). It is, in principle, a good thing to get a wife (Prov. 18:22), but whether you should remarry or not is a question of prudence and wisdom.

Megan and I had talked about the possibility of remarriage long before she died. We were clear: if one died before the other, the remaining spouse should get remarried. Not that it matters too much (except in our own minds!), but I had Megan's permission. She had mine. Christian, can I advise you to have this sort of conversation with your husband or wife? It may help you one day.

So, I was free to remarry, but *should* I? To be honest, in the early days after Megan's death, I didn't feel adequately equipped to look after a new wife (let alone find one!). That would change later, but not then. If you're pondering remarriage, ask yourself: What challenges might remarriage bring? Am I ready to be remarried? These questions are a good place to start.

Question Two: 'Is it too soon to get remarried?'
This is the most debated question around this topic. Why? Because everybody and their sister has an opinion. I'm serious. Think about what you've said or heard: 'Wow, she's getting remarried already? It's only been—!' Or how about: 'It's been —

already. Why hasn't he got married again?' Sound familiar? The problem is: the — is different for everyone.

Let me respond to the question of timing in two ways. First, recognise that when to remarry is a question of wisdom. If your intended 'belongs to the Lord,' there's no right or wrong answer about *when* to get married. You could get hitched tomorrow. That's not the question. This is a decision to be undertaken with careful thinking, sincere consideration of those involved and much prayer. The question: is this the *proper* time?

Secondly, because you aren't always the ideal judge of what's best, lean into your church family and especially your elders. Ask questions like: 'Do you think I'm ready to be remarried?"What concerns do you have about me getting remarried?' 'How would you advise me to proceed?' 'Plans are established by seeking advice; so if you wage war, obtain guidance' (Prov. 20:18). Seek advice from godly people.

A sad admission: as I moved closer to remarriage, I didn't always do the things I'm advocating. I pressed forward with my agenda more than I care to admit. I *did* ask for help from godly people in my life, but I didn't always appreciate their counsel. Learn from my mistakes. You will be thankful for wise counsel. 'Plans fail for lack of counsel, but with many advisors they succeed' (Prov. 15:22). If your elders advise slowing down, do it. If they recommend pulling the plug for a season, listen and learn. You don't always know what you need best. Especially not with a decision this weighty! So think carefully and entrust yourself to the spiritual leaders God has put into your life. Together you can assess: 'Is it too soon to get remarried?'

Question Three: 'How will I ever find someone?'

I don't know! Neither do you. But we can trust God to provide according to His good plan. God provides godly spouses: 'Houses and wealth are inherited from parents, but a prudent wife is from the Lord' (Prov. 19:14). Whilst this is true, we can be proactive in pursuing a spouse or putting ourselves in the way of where we could meet a potential husband or wife. My advice: consider your wider friendship group and church networks. Do you know of anyone with potential? If not, don't be afraid to ask godly people who know you well to consider whether they know anyone who might serve as a suitable spouse.

Isn't this the ideal way: entrust yourself to godly people and let them make an introduction? Just be careful along the way to avoid despair: 'I'll never find someone.' You don't know that. God is sovereign over the hearts of men in their romantic relationships just as much as he's sovereign over the hearts of rulers in their governing of nations (Prov. 21:1). Trust Him to give you what you need when you need it, even if it's not what you want and when you want it.

Question Four: 'How will the children respond?'

This question is so terribly personal that it's impossible to answer. But it's one you *must* think through well. I don't know how your children will handle the thought of you remarrying. They may be angry or overjoyed. They may find it uncomfortable, or they might be pleased as punch. As I even began to broach the topic of remarriage with my children, I had all of these responses and then some! One child didn't want me

189

to even say the word 'marriage!' He just found it too weird. So much depends upon the number, ages, and temperaments of your children.

My counsel then: communicate early and often. Ask a lot of questions of the children (relative to their age and understanding). Be patient if your children don't immediately think the same way you do. Time and open dialogue can be a real help. You do not want to exasperate your children on this point: 'Fathers, do not exasperate your children; instead, bring them up in the training and instruction of the Lord' (Eph. 6:4). But you can certainly also expect some folly: 'Folly is bound up in the heart of a child' (Prov. 22:15). You've got to train them in how to think in a godly way about this.

You can do this by asking a lot of questions of your children. What do they think about you remarrying? Were you to remarry, what would be hard? What might be good? As you get closer to remarrying, discuss the potential spouse, how things are working and might work should you get married. Try to anticipate trouble spots, and talk about them. In one sense, you want to take Peter's advice to husbands and apply it to your parenting: 'Be considerate as you live with' your children. (1 Pet. 3:7) Above all though, you have to be willing to move slowly. This will be hard. But patience and deliberateness pay off: 'Desire without knowledge is not good – how much more will hasty feet miss the way!' (Prov. 19:2) A good rule of thumb: slow down.

Question Five: 'Will I compare the two?'

This question bothers those considering remarriage. Most widowers truly don't want to compare their first and second wives. Either way, fight for contentment today and everyday, whether or not you're remarried, and whether or not you tend to compare. To put it crassly (in the words of Stephen Stills) 'Love the one you're with.' The Bible says it better: 'The fear of the Lord leads to life; then one rests content, untouched by trouble' (Prov. 19:23).

Fear the Lord and be thankful for the spouse He's given you today. What you want to steer clear of is vocally comparing the two. Never say things like: 'My first wife never used to do that.' I can think of few quicker ways to anger or ostracise your second wife. Don't allow your children to make such comparisons either. If you do compare them in your mind, make sure what you are thinking is true, right, pure, admirable or praiseworthy (Phil. 4:8). As you guard your thoughts, guard you tongue. 'Those who guard their lips preserve their lives, but those who speak rashly will come to ruin' (Prov. 13:3).

Those five questions are a start. Let me underscore yet again how important it is to solicit the input of your elders. God has gifted his church with godly men to help shepherd the church. Are you humble enough to ask for help?

Let me close by finishing our family's story on this point. I said earlier that I wanted to remarry, but what I didn't say is that, as of writing this, I am remarried. Praise God.

The potted history: about a year after Megan's death, Naomi and I began to consider whether we should pursue a relationship. Our families had been friends for some time, but we began to consider what sort of future there might be for us. Over time, our love grew, and in God's kindness, Naomi and I were married eighteen months later. What a brave woman she is. What a delight our marriage is.

Let me underscore that last point. You might be tempted to think our marriage is purely one of convenience. It's not – as our family, church family, and friends know. God has given us a delightful marriage. It didn't come easy. Along the way, we sought input, aimed to take it slow, and did our best to shepherd the children through the process. We talked and talked and talked through everything!

As a family, we haven't finished the race yet but, by God's grace, we're running well so far. God has been very kind to us. Of course we miss Megan, but Naomi and I are lovingly committed to one another for as long as He gives us. We have to trust the Lord when considering remarriage and, of course, trust Him in marriage. 'Give thanks to the Lord, for he is good; his love endures forever' (Ps. 107:1).

31) The ache

I sit writing this, and I'm three and a half years on from Megan's death. I've said this before, but writing this has taken ages! In God's providence though, the amount of time it's taken to write this has been beneficial for me. I trust time has given me some perspective. Life has certainly come and gone. Of course, God's faithfulness has continued. The thing is: so much has changed! Our lives today feel so very different from those early days. One thing that time definitely has given me: more opportunities to miss Megan. What do I mean?

Just over three years ago, our daughter won her year group's sports day race. She nailed it! Funny enough, I missed it – I was collecting our younger son from nursery. Thanks to a kind friend, we have it on video! Megan would have loved to have seen this.

Nearly two years ago, our son started reception. As he walked into school for the first time, holding his big brother's hand, my heart ached. Not so much because he was growing up. You would think that, wouldn't you? No, I ached because Megan would have loved to have seen it, but she didn't.

Then, just last week, our eldest son finished his GCSE's. It's an important educational milestone. He worked hard, and he weathered the pressure well. We'll see how his grades turn out, but we're pretty sure he'll do alright. For me, this day brought both joy and sadness. Megan would have wanted to be here to celebrate with him. I took him out for Korean takeaway to mark the day; I reckon we both sensed her absence. Of course we did. Not only is she not there to see it, but the children and I aren't able to enjoy those moments with her.

I ache for Megan regularly. And, of course, it's not just the big moments. Countless trivial occurrences bring similar grief:

- Someone describes, in a podcast, how invaluable mums are, especially one's birth mum is. Ooof
- I hear a happy couple talk about celebrating their 15-year anniversary. Megan and I didn't quite make it to 15 years. Ach
- A woman asked us (when I was taking all the children swimming): 'Where's mum today, kids? She's having a lie in, I hope, as dad's got you all out for swim.' Ouch
- At bedtime, our 3-year-old says innocently: 'My mummy's in heaven with Jesus.' Ugh

Hear me clearly: I didn't ache for Megan because people are insensitive – the podcaster, the happy couple, the woman at the pool and, of course, our 3-year-old have no fault here at all! Mercifully, I don't think we told the woman at the pool the whole story. We just smiled and nodded.

Fact is: you shouldn't read this and be afraid to talk about your life in front of a widower! This way of thinking is akin to single people in the church being angry and feeling slighted that pastors (and Scripture) speak *mostly* to married people.

Scripture is pretty certain single people are sensible and can make application to their own lives! Widows and widowers need not be offended that people aren't always thinking of them and their sorrows. We all must be aware of envy here. The truth is, I ache for Megan because she isn't here, and countless normal-life moments have and do remind me of her. I miss her still, even almost four years on.

I ache. We ache. It's worth saying: this ache isn't wrong. In fact, it's to-be-expected.

Our ache reminds us of our sin and its consequences. In Genesis 3, God told Adam that he would surely die. 'Dust you are and to dust you will return" (Gen. 3:19). As Adam, our covenant head goes, so we all go. Despite the claims of the serpent, our sin is lethal. We all are living now, but we will all die. Many have died before us, and unless Jesus delays, many more will die after us. There is 'a time to be born and a time to die' (Ecc. 3:2).

We should expect this ache, and it is, if rightly used, profitable. Death can and should prompt us to turn to Jesus, the second and greater Adam, in whom we find life: 'For the wages of sin is death, but the gift of God is eternal life in Christ Jesus our Lord' (Rom. 6:23). Yet though the Christian finds forgiveness and eternal life in the covenant of grace, the ache still persists. I know it does for me.

As we deal with our pain, these two certainties provide comfort and assurance:

First, God is aware of my aches, and He is with me in them. 'Precious in the sight of the Lord is the death of his faithful

195

servants' (Ps. 116:15). Something that's 'precious' to us, is something that we treasure.

God doesn't treat the death of his faithful servants carelessly. Megan's death was precious in God's sight. As her death is precious, so too is its impact. God is aware of my aches. He's aware of the painful walk into reception, and He's aware of the woman at the pool. 'Yet the Lord longs to be gracious to you; therefore he will rise up to show you compassion. For the Lord is a God of justice. Blessed are all who wait for him!' (Is. 30:18).

But God is not merely moved with compassion in my heartache, He is also firmly with me in my pain. He was with Israel during her exile in Babylon, and He would be with her when He brought her out. These promises have clear application to all God's people:

> When you pass through the waters, I will be with you; and when you pass through the rivers, they will not sweep over you. When you walk through the fire, you will not be burned; the flames will not set you ablaze. For I am the Lord your God, the Holy One of Israel, your Saviour ... Since you are precious and honoured in my sight, and because I love you, I will give people in exchange for you, nations in exchange for your life. Do not be afraid, for I am with you; I will bring your children from the east and gather you from the west (Is. 43:2–5).

Do you hear that 'precious' language again? God is always with us. The 'ache' may be there, but it will not destroy us. Why? Because the Holy One of Israel, our Saviour is with us. We need not be afraid. He loves us, and will always be with us. We don't ache alone. Isn't this comforting?

Second, my ache will end. This has been a constant theme in these pages. And rightly so. This life is painful, but this life will soon be over. This life is filled with weeping, but we will not always weep. Jesus said:

> Very truly I tell you, you will weep and mourn while the world rejoices. You will grieve, but your grief will turn to joy. A woman giving birth to a child has pain because her time has come; but when her baby is born she forgets the anguish because of her joy that a child is born into the world. So with you: now is your time of grief, but I will see you again and you will rejoice, and no one will take away your joy (Jn. 16:20–22).

I'd ask you to imagine a world without death, grieving and the ache, but you can't do it. Our more normal sorrows and corresponding joys (labour and childbirth) give us a glimpse into what it must be like, but we still can't fathom it. Hear these words again: 'You will rejoice, and no one will take away your joy.' Amazing. Wonderful. Good. That day is coming, friends.

God is with us now. But in that day, He will dwell with us in fullness.

> And I heard a loud voice from the throne saying, 'Look! God's dwelling-place is now among the people, and he will dwell with them. They will be his people, and God himself will be with them and be their God. He will wipe every tear from their eyes. There will be no more death or mourning or crying or pain, for the old order of things has passed away' (Rev. 21:3–4).

What a day that will be! No more ache! Not even a twinge.

Brothers and sisters, God has promised it, and it will come to pass. You ache now, but you won't then. The old order of things will pass away. No more: 'Ooof,' 'Ach,' 'Ouch,' 'Ugh' or 'Argh.' Not a one. Never again.

If God gives me a few more years, these three and a half years will give way to 20 or 40. It will pass like a breath. It has already. I know that the children and I will still ache. It may mute slightly, but I reckon it will occasionally return with a fervour. And rightly so.

But amidst the ache in that day and every day, we will have all the comfort and assurance we need:

> But Christ has indeed been raised from the dead, the firstfruits of those who have fallen asleep. For since death came through a man, the resurrection of the dead comes also through a man. For as in Adam all die, so in Christ all will be made alive. But each in turn: Christ, the firstfruits; then, when he comes, those who belong to him. Then the end will come, when he hands over the kingdom to God the Father after he has destroyed all dominion, authority and power. For he must reign until he has put all his enemies under his feet. The last enemy to be destroyed is death (1 Cor. 15:20–26).

Praise be to God. Though we ache today, our resurrected Saviour will bring this day to close and usher in a new and better day.

32) Our prophet, priest and king

Jesus Christ transforms our grief. He definitely did and still does for our family.

What do I mean? Jesus was in the background of our days on the critical care ward. Our tears and our uncertainties were shaped by His righteous life and substitutionary death. He was our strength in the early days after Megan's death. Our days and nights were changed by His powerful resurrection and ongoing intercession. He is our hope still – even now, years later. We look forward to His bodily return, His sure judgment and His ushering in of a new age. Jesus was and is and will be all in all.

The story and the reflections running through these pages start and finish with Him. He deserves all the glory for anything good reflected here. 'Not to us, Lord, not to us but to your name be the glory, because of your love and faithfulness' (Ps. 115:1). In this closing reflection, I want to underscore the way Jesus transforms grief.

Question 23 of the Westminster Shorter Catechism asks: 'What offices does Christ execute as our Redeemer?' The answer: 'Christ as our Redeemer, executes the offices of a Prophet, of a Priest, and of a King, both in his estate of humiliation and exaltation.'

Time and again, this catechism smashes it for presenting biblical truth with clarity and simplicity. When you've got teaching as good as this catechism, why reinvent the wheel? I want to expound upon our Saviour according to his three offices, and show how the Lord Jesus shapes our grief as prophet, priest and king.

Jesus is our prophet.

God promised in Deuteronomy 18:18: 'I will raise up for them a prophet like you [Moses] from among their fellow Israelites, and I will put my words in his mouth. He will tell them everything I command him.' Over the years, Israel had many prophets, but none was quite up to scratch. None, that is, until Jesus.

> In the past God spoke to our ancestors through the prophets at many times and in various ways, but in these last days he has spoken to us by his Son, whom he appointed heir of all things, and through whom also he made the universe (Heb. 1:1–2).

Jesus, the Son of God, spoke for God, and yet He did more. 'The Son is the radiance of God's glory and the exact representation of his being' (Heb. 1:3). Jesus perfectly and conclusively speaks for God.

How does Jesus, as our prophet, transform our grief?

Firstly, during our losses and sorrows, God sometimes seems silent. We may pray and feel like God isn't hearing us. 'Why won't God speak to me? Why won't He answer my questions – or at least give me a word of comfort?' These questions are understandable, but maybe we feel like God hasn't spoken to us because we're listening for the wrong thing? We shouldn't expect God to speak audibly to us. He's told us all we need to hear in the Bible. Don't underestimate the ability of Jesus, through the Scriptures, to comfort our weary souls. Jesus says to you today,:'Come to me, all you who are weary and burdened, and I will give you rest' (Mt. 11:28). We need to listen to Him.

Secondly, Jesus give us understanding. There is so much, in difficult times, that we *don't* know. 'How will we pay the bills? How will I raise a newborn? How will the children react to losing their mum? How will I survive without Megan's tamale pies?' So many questions go unanswered. Yet, as our prophet, Jesus tells and shows what we *need* to know. Jesus as God reveals God. And He also explains *me*. He rightly explains our world and our sufferings. Jesus is the interpretive key to life's most pressing questions. He comforts us in our sorrows, admonishes us in our sin, directs us back to the Father and instructs us how we should then live. We need to listen to Him.

Will you listen to Jesus? His Word is sufficient in your grief. It really is all you need. 'His divine power has given us *everything we need* for a godly life through our knowledge of him who called us by his own glory and goodness' (2 Pet. 1:3, italics added). Will you go to Him for comfort?

But Jesus doesn't only comfort. He also directs us in our grief. Will you let Jesus' words direct you in your suffering? 'Whoever has my commands and keeps them is the one who loves me. The one who loves me will be loved by my Father, and I too will love them and show myself to them" (Jn. 14:21). Do you want to see more of Jesus, even in your grief? Then obey His commands. Listen to, learn from, be comforted by and obey Jesus. He is our prophet.

Jesus is our priest.

We're separated from God by our sin. We have in Adam broken covenant with God. And we have ourselves broken God's law. We live and breathe under His just wrath (Jn. 3:36), awaiting final judgement. Since Eden, there's been a vast gulf between holy God and sinful man.

We feel this gulf acutely amidst our grief. All sufferings are a result of humanity's sin, and the pain we experience reminds us that all is not right with the world. All is not right with God.

Thankfully, Jesus as our priest sets things right. In the covenant of grace, Jesus as the second Adam reconciles holy God and sinful man. As our priest, Jesus lived a righteous life and, in his death, bore God's wrath for sinners. 'For Christ also suffered once for sins, the righteous for the unrighteous, to bring you to God' (1 Pet. 3:18). As our priest, Jesus brings us into God's presence and intercedes for us before the Father. All of this, He does, by His grace, for the elect – all who place their faith in Him (Eph. 2:8–9).

How does Jesus, as our priest, transform our grief?

Firstly, Jesus addresses our greatest need. This fundamentally changes how I view my grief. Job loss, the death of a loved one, a broken bone, betrayal by a friend – it all hurts. But none of it is my greatest problem. Jesus has atoned for my sin once and for all. 'And so Jesus also suffered ... to make the people holy through his own blood' (Heb. 13:12). If these sufferings bring with them a cloud of sorrow – and sometimes it's a thick cloud! – then Jesus' atoning sacrifice punches holes of light through the clouds. The clouds may remain, but they will not last forever. Light has broken through, and a brighter day awaits. To understand my grief, I must look back to the cross and Jesus' priestly work.

Secondly, Jesus guarantees my acceptance before God. God sometimes felt distant after Megan died. I was even tempted to wonder if He was angry with me. Thankfully, Jesus' priesthood addresses these concerns. Because of Jesus, I know what God thinks about me. I am a 'dearly loved child' (Eph. 5:1). Through Jesus' atoning sacrifice I'm a child of God! I can endure hardship by seeing trials as fatherly 'discipline' (Heb. 12:7). If I'm going to grieve well, I must look back to the cross and Jesus' priestly work.

Thirdly, I can go to God for real help. I am not merely promised heaven one day. I can go to God today. Jesus has purchased this access for me:

> Therefore, since we have a great high priest who has ascended into heaven, Jesus the Son of God ... Let us then approach God's throne of grace with confidence, so that we may receive mercy and find grace to help us in our time of need (Heb. 4:14–16).

Through the Holy Spirit's empowerment, there is grace available to me. I just need to ask. I am not hopeless and helpless in my loss. I have mercy and grace to respond well to my grief, but I must look back to the cross and Jesus' priestly work.

Will the cross shape your bereavement? Or will your bereavement shape your view of God? The question really is as straightforward as that. Read those two questions again. Christian, all things in life (even our greatest sorrows) take on a different hue in light of Jesus' priestly work. Lean into your great high priest. He is your salvation and your help today.

Jesus is our king.

> For to us a child is born, to us a son is given, and the government will be on his shoulders. And he will be called Wonderful Counsellor, Mighty God, Everlasting Father, Prince of Peace. Of the greatness of his government and peace there will be no end. He will reign on David's throne and over his kingdom, establishing and upholding it with justice and righteousness from that time on and for ever. The zeal of the Lord Almighty will accomplish this (Is. 9:6–7).

We read this at Christmas, but do you see what it promises? A king. A king who would be both God and man. A righteous ruler who would reign for ever and ever.

Jesus is that promised king. He is the eternal Son of God made man, the king forever. Pilate queried His royal credentials, and Jesus pulled no punches: 'My kingdom is not of this world' (Jn. 18:36). He who came to this world as a servant has been raised to new life that He might reign forever as king. True enough, His kingdom is not of this world. But it will be one day. 'For he must reign until he has put all his enemies under his feet' (1 Cor. 15:25). End of story: Jesus is and will be our king.

How does Jesus, our king, transform our grief?

204

Firstly, King Jesus has charge over *everything*. My wife's death wasn't a surprise to Him. His plan is still being worked out, and it will be good. I couldn't always see this in the moment, and sometimes I still struggle to see it. I have to live by faith in my king, not by what I see (Heb. 11:1). If Jesus really is the promised king, and if His reign really will one day be total, then I have to trust in Him today. I must willingly submit to His good plan for me. 'Humble yourselves, therefore, under God's mighty hand, that he may lift you up in due time. Cast all your anxiety on him because he cares for you' (1 Pet. 5:6–7). My king may bring me through a deep valley today, but He will bring me up again in His good time. I can and must trust my king.

Secondly, this world, and all its sin, stinks. You know it does. My grief and your grief are a part of this. But it will be put right one day even if we struggle to see this now. This is where the book of Revelation can help us. Revelation gives a heavenly view of our world from the time of the apostles until the end of the age. Our world spins on as the wonder and all the heartache continues. All the while, today and everyday, Revelation tells us: Jesus reigns as both the lion and lamb. Jesus is the regal, conquering lion, and He's the sacrificial lamb who has been slain but is now alive again. The beings in the heavenly throne room get what we so often miss: 'Worthy is the Lamb, who was slain, to receive power and wealth and wisdom and strength and honour and glory and praise!' (Rev. 5:12) Oh, our world rages. But the Lamb has conquered. His victory is already won. He merely needs to return and claim His prize. All will be well one day. Jesus guarantees it. I can and must trust my king.

Jesus has told me what I am: a sinner who deserves God's righteous judgment. Jesus has made atonement for me. In Him, by faith, I am justified, forgiven and free to live unto God. I still sin and disobey my king. But my king is gracious and kind.

Hear me as I close: Christians don't grieve perfectly. We will need to repent in and through our grief – all the while, looking to Jesus. I hope that my children see this in me: 'Our daddy didn't grieve perfectly. But he repented a lot, and he trusted in Jesus.' I hope that you, dear reader, see this in me as well, especially here at the end of these reflections. Look to Jesus, repent often and grieve well.

Our prophet, priest and king is our only hope. Jesus is the sinner's best friend, as John Newton reminds us:

> One there is, above all others,
> Well deserves the name of Friend;
> His is love beyond a brother's,
> Costly, free, and knows no end:
> They who once his kindness prove,
> Find it everlasting love!
>
> Which of all our friends to save us,
> Could or would have shed their blood?
> But our Jesus died to have us
> Reconciled in him to God:
> This was boundless love indeed!
> Jesus is a Friend in need.

O for grace our hearts to soften!
Teach us, Lord, at length to love.
We, alas, forget too often,
What a Friend we have above.
But when home our souls are brought,
We will love thee as we ought.

when sorrows like sea billows roll

Conclusion
Sanctified and Sanctifying

You grieve. We all do. We lose things we love, and we feel torn up about it. Our grief needs to be sanctified.

> Therefore, with minds that are alert and fully sober, set your hope on the grace to be brought to you when Jesus Christ is revealed at his coming. As obedient children, do not conform to the evil desires you had when you lived in ignorance. But just as he who called you is holy, so be holy in all you do; for it is written: 'Be holy, because I am holy' (1 Pet. 1:13–16).

Hopefully, in these pages, you've found help to this end, a guidebook to grieving well by one who's gone before. Maybe now, you can say: 'It is well with my soul.'

I've never been in a boat at sea. The closest I've come was a nautical tour of Portsmouth harbour a few years ago! I began by saying that experiencing grief is like being in a storm at sea. Is it really? Well, you don't have to take my word for it. God says it is. In Psalm 107, the writer gives us four stereotypical vignettes of how God rescues His people. With an obvious forward look to the Lord Jesus Christ, one is a rescue at sea. It's a Psalm meant to drive the people of God to thanksgiving.

23 Some went out on the sea in ships;

they were merchants on the mighty waters.

24 They saw the works of the Lord,

his wonderful deeds in the deep.

25 For he spoke and stirred up a tempest

that lifted high the waves.

26 They mounted up to the heavens and went down to the depths;

in their peril their courage melted away.

27 They reeled and staggered like drunkards;

they were at their wits' end.

28 Then they cried out to the Lord in their trouble,

and he brought them out of their distress.

29 He stilled the storm to a whisper;

the waves of the sea were hushed.

30 They were glad when it grew calm,

and he guided them to their desired haven.

31 Let them give thanks to the Lord for his unfailing love

and his wonderful deeds for mankind.

32 Let them exalt him in the assembly of the people

and praise him in the council of the elders.

(Ps. 107:23–32)

This is what grief feels like. You're sailing along, and God sovereignly stirs up a tempest. You lose someone or something. The waves of loss crash in. Your courage wanes as your sorrows grow. Verse 27 is the experience of so many: they reel and stagger like drunkards, and they're at their wits end.

Notice what those caught up in the storm do: they grieve in the right direction. They cry out to the Lord in their distress. That's the first step in sanctifying grief.

In this moment, there are so many possible poor responses:

- Check out as fast as possible. Seek simple, inadequate comforts. Many do this; some even contemplate the ultimate 'escape' of taking their own life
- Act like the grief isn't there. Play the 'tough guy' who pretends like nothing's wrong when so much clearly is
- Take it passively. Do nothing and, in the process, be carried along simply and unthinkingly by grief

These sailors on the storms of grief don't do any of that. They move toward God. In the moment of grief, there are so many possible godly responses:

- See your loss and your grief accurately. Admit that it is devastating and it does hurt
- Remember who God is and what part He plays in your grief. He rules over the wind and the waves. He's ultimately your Saviour, the Lord Jesus Christ
- Slow down enough to ask difficult questions: How can I grow in godliness through this? What does this loss show me about myself?

The irony is that the illustration breaks down. The sailor in the storm really only has two choices: give up or do the best he can. And, of course, that's often how our lives feel. We're just going to do the best we can. Fair enough. Some very good sailors have been brought down by the waves of grief. We recognise that.

But maybe, just maybe, we can grow *in* our grieving. Maybe we can grow *through* our grief. So often, we wrongly think that sanctification *merely* happens when we pray, hear a good sermon or have a chat with a Christian brother or sister. But let's not kid ourselves, true Christian growth often happens most in the hard things of life, hard things like grief.

Did you notice how this section of Psalm 107 ends? 'Then they cried out to the Lord in their trouble, and he brought them out of their distress. He stilled the storm to a whisper; the waves of the sea were hushed. They were glad when it grew calm, and he guided them to their desired haven' (Ps. 107:28–30). God does bring His people out of their distress. He may do so in this life, or He may do so in the next. But God does eventually bring every storm to a 'whisper.' He does bring His people into their 'desired haven' – now or in eternity. One day, there will be no more sorrows like sea billows.

In light of this sure and certain outcome, let us do as the Psalmist commands: 'Let them give thanks to the Lord for his unfailing love and his wonderful deeds for mankind. Let them exalt him in the assembly of the people and praise him in the council of the elders' (Ps. 107:31–32).

We miss Megan. We wish she were still here. But we can, by the power of the Holy Spirit, thank God both for her life and for the growth He has and will bring about in us through her death. We can grieve well. We can say: 'It is well with our souls.' Praise God.

Acknowledgements

God has been good to me – both in the circumstances of my life and in the writing of this book. I want to express my thanks to those whom God has used to help this book come into being.

A big 'thank you' goes to the St Giles church family. How privileged I am to serve the Lord with you. In our shared lives, in our mutual encouragement, in our love for each other, and even in our grieving together, we have seen the 'manifold wisdom of God' (Eph. 3:10). Praise God. You are all over the story of this book, and in countless ways you helped it come into being – not least of all through your prayers. This book is, fittingly, dedicated to you.

Aaron – what can I say? Thank you for being in the hospital all day and all night. You know better than most how uncomfortable those sofas are! Thank you for your sarcasm (most of the time) and thank you for your enduring friendship. You are a good shepherd and you cared for me. Without your support and wise input, this book would never have come to be. It's a privilege to still be serving alongside you. Thank you.

John, Pete and Windsor – thank you for your friendship and for giving me all the time I needed to care for my family. I'm thankful for you and your steady service to our church family.

To my parents and in-laws – Dad and Mama, Byron and Angela, Stuart and Anna – Thank you. Whether near or far, you have helped us in countless ways. Your encouragement, prayers, help and influence are behind this book. I love you. Thank you. And to all of our extended family – brothers and sisters, all of the in-laws, uncles and aunts, cousins, nephews and nieces – thank you for all of your prayers and support.

I feel compelled here, one last time, to thank again all of those who prayed for us or helped us practically around the time of Megan's death. Churches were praying for us. Friends set up crowdfunding initiatives. Christians nearby did so much to help keep us afloat – not least of all making us a steady stream of meals. For all of that and so much more, thank you.

I am grateful for my friend Andrew and all at Grace Publications (especially Helen) for their support and for seeing this book through to publication. A special thanks goes to those who read this book in advance and helped make it better – Alex, James (ever my wingman), Mike, Stuart, Alan and Rebecca.

Luke, Stephen, Peter, Justus, Georgiana, Michael and Euan – as promised, you're named in the end! Thank you for asking about the book, being excited about it, and putting up with my distracted mind while writing it. I love you, and I am so grateful to God for you. In large part, this book is for you.

Naomi – without your belief that this book was important, without your prodding to keep writing, without your sacrificing of time in the diary, and without your daily, affectionate encouragement in all areas of life, there's no way this book would have been written. Thank you. I love you. We never could have planned this, could we? Yet here we are. God has been very kind to us. Shall we keep going for as many years as God gives us?

when sorrows like sea billows roll

Scripture Index

218